This book given to

_____

On the occasion of

_____

presented by

_____

_____

date

DEVOTIONS

for the *Chronologically*

Gifted

Edited by Les Bayer

CPH
SAINT LOUIS

Cover photo credits (clockwise from top right): © R. Kaufman/The Stock Market; Image Studios/Index Stock Imagery; Telegraph Colour Library/FPG International; J. Feingersh/The Stock Market; T. & D. McCarthy/The Stock Market; back cover: Telegraph Colour Library/FPG International.

The quotation on page 36 is from *The Book of Concord,* Theodore G. Tappert, ed. (Philadelphia: Fortress Press, 1983), 310. Used by permission.

Hymn stanzas taken from *Lutheran Worship* © 1982 Concordia Publishing House. Used with permission.

Quotations from *The Small Catechism* by Martin Luther © 1986 Concordia Publishing House. Used with permission.

All Scripture quotations, unless otherwise indicated, are taken from the HOLY BIBLE, NEW INTERNATIONAL VERSION®. NIV®. Copyright © 1973, 1978, 1984 by International Bible Society. Used by permission of Zondervan Publishing House. All rights reserved.

Scripture quotations marked KJV are from the King James or Authorized Version of the Bible.

Scripture quotations marked NKJV are from the Holy Bible, New King James Version, copyright © 1979, 1980, 1982 Thomas Nelson, Inc. Used by permission.

Scripture quotations marked RSV are from the Revised Standard Version of the Bible, copyrighted 1946, 1952, © 1971, 1973 by the Division of Christian Education of the National Council of the Churches of Christ in the U.S.A., and are used by permission.

Scripture quotations marked NRSV are from the New Revised Standard Version of the Bible, copyright © 1989. Used by permission.

Scripture quotations marked TEV are from the Good News Bible, the Bible in TODAY'S ENGLISH VERSION. Copyright © American Bible Society, 1966, 1971, 1976. Used by permission.

Library of Congress Cataloging-in-Publication Data
Devotions for the chronologically gifted/edited by Les Bayer.
     p. cm.
   ISBN 0-570-05358-7
   1. Aged Prayer-books and devotion—English.   I. Bayer, Les.
BV4580.D45   1999
242´.65—dc21   99-32402
                                           CIP

1 2 3 4 5 6 7 8 9 10   08 07 06 05 04 03 02 01 00 99

Contents

Devotions
for the
Chronologically
Gifted

Introduction

After I finished college, I never lived closer to my dad's home than 400 miles. During the last 35 years of his life, when I was able to visit him, he always asked me to read the daily devotion.

I noticed that several of his devotional booklets had pages that looked worn and used. He obviously had read these devotions many times. Other pages and even entire booklets looked as if they had never been used. As I read some of the unused ones, I realized that they had not been written with the older person in mind. Amazingly, some of the little-used materials had been written for seniors. After careful reading, I realized these dealt almost exclusively with death and dying. While my father said he was interested in death, he was more interested in how to live and in the lives of those around him.

As years went by and he moved from retirement to "retiring from retirement," I noticed that my father had torn out some of the worn devotions and put them into his Bible. My father lived to be 101. One of the great blessings he received throughout his life was a clear mind. In fact, I spoke to him over the phone several hours before his death. He told me that he didn't "feel real good" and thought he might be getting the flu.

My experience with my father caused me to believe that there is a great need and opportunity to develop devotional materials that reflect the real lifestyles of seniors. I contacted people who have been working successfully in ministries involving seniors, and I contacted seniors who have successfully moved into retirement. I asked these individuals to write devotional thoughts for the "chronologically gifted." They've written about the joys, concerns, sorrows, opportunities, fears, faith, and blessings of the senior child of God. My prayer is that what they have written will provide help and encouragement during your first reading and that some of the pages will become worn from your repeated use.

I want to say a special thank you to all those who did the writing; to Fred Meyer and Frank Starr, who helped with the editing; to Ruth Geisler, former editor at Concordia Publishing House, Dawn Weinstock, and Edward Grube for their advice and help; to Carol Smithe, who read my horrible handwriting as she did the typing; and to my wife, Lois, who has demonstrated in her life so many of the retirement joys described in this book.

In the book, *Angels Can Fly because They Take Themselves Lightly* (Concordia 1992), Rich Bimler quotes a prayer that he heard at a conference. I feel it's a prayer that has some reminders for all seniors. It describes the negatives to avoid. It also provides a good introduction to the devotions that follow and the positive life of the Christian senior as described by the writers in this book.

Lord, Thou knowest better than I know myself that I am growing older and will someday be old. Keep me from the fatal habit of thinking I must say something on every subject and on every occasion. Release me from craving to straighten out everyone's affairs. Make me thoughtful but not moody, helpful but not bossy. With my vast store of wisdom, it seems a pity not to use it all, but Thou knowest, Lord, that I want a few friends at the end.

Keep my mind free from the recital of endless details; give me the wings to get to the point. Seal my lips on my aches and pains. They are increasing, and love of rehearsing them is becoming sweeter as the years go by. I dare not ask for grace enough to enjoy the talk of other's pains, but help me to endure them with patience.

I do not ask for an improved memory but for a growing humility and a lessening cocksureness when my memory seems to clash with the memories of others. Teach me the glorious lesson that occasionally I may be mistaken.

Keep me reasonably sweet; I don't want to be a saint—some of them are so hard to live with—but a sour old person is one of the crowning works of the devil. Give me the ability to see good things in unexpected people. And give me, Lord, the grace to tell them so. Amen.

Les Bayer

My Most Difficult Job

The Spirit's presence is shown in some way in each person for the good of all.

1 Corinthians 12:7 (TEV)

Arvilla was one of my teachers. I was helping her because, after a lot of health and family problems, she had entered a nursing home. Like so many other people, she had said she would never go to a home. However, there was no choice. Her family packed her up and delivered her to the front door, then they phoned me.

My job, per family instructions, was to help Arvilla accept reality and to tell her to quit complaining. I went with my own agenda because I love Arvilla as a sister in Christ. When I arrived, she did not complain, and I discovered that she had accepted reality. We talked about her new home and the scheduled events. She already knew several people. As I was leaving, Arvilla said, "Of all the jobs I've had in life, the most difficult one is being a little old lady."

Her words echoed in my ears as I drove home. When I was in school, I knew that my job was being a student. It didn't pay anything, but it occupied my time and energy, which made it an occupation. Arvilla made me realize that there was a job on the other side of those that paid a salary. "Being an old person" would occupy my time and energy in the future as it was right now for Arvilla.

Many years ago, I figured out that I learned more about being a student or a pastor from those who *did* these tasks than from the experts who *talked* about them. As I planned for my old-age occupation, I determined to learn from those who already had the job. As I thought of the old people in my life, I realized that I had plenty of teachers.

Some didn't like their jobs as old people. They complained, blamed others, and refused to adjust to the job description of their new occupation. Because they weren't getting paid to be old, they didn't have to do a good job. Nobody could fire them.

Others were glad they were still alive. They weren't doing the job for the pay. They were doing it because it was their station in life. Their age was a gift from God. They had been blessed. Therefore, they could be a blessing to others. They did a good job at being old because age was their gift.

I liked the spirituality I saw in those who did a good job at being old. Among others, these individuals helped me identify a deeper application of the Gospel of Jesus Christ. I grew up knowing Jesus had died for my sins. He had saved me. It was a great discovery when I understood that He had died for everyone else too. Not only does He save people that I love—which is great—

but He also forgives those whom I don't like. His forgiveness takes away my need to hurt. The faults of others don't pull me down because Christ has forgiven them too. It's a group plan. Just as Christ has forgiven me, He has forgiven others too.

The Gospel has still another blessing for us. Christ made us saints even while we are sinners. We don't act completely holy now, but holiness is a future certainty. We may not always like things about ourselves, but Jesus accepts us because He died to forgive our sins.

We don't need forgiveness for being old; we do need to know that we are accepted and *acceptable* as old people. By the time we are old enough to say we are old, we have learned many lessons—lessons that younger people can learn from us.

When we were younger, we did not earn the love of God or the love of our family and friends through hard work and achievements during our productive years. We were important to God for no earthly reason. He loved us simply because He loved us! He accepted us for Jesus' sake. Our family and friends accepted us because we used our time and ability to contribute to others. We were important because of our relationship with others and their relationship with us.

Our occupation as elderly people offers similar opportunities. As we grow older, we may depend on someone to drive us places, to shop for us, to dress us, and even to feed us. These are not evils that need forgiveness. They are conditions in a sinful, damaged world that we tolerate. Others often accept our needs and want to help us. Our job is to help them enjoy helping us.

An important secret of doing a good job as an old person is to make people glad that you're still alive. Some people have to take care of you. It's their job. That doesn't mean they do it only for pay. Most professional caregivers do it because they want to. They like old people, and they are learning how to grow old. Even those who are doing the job only for the paycheck could change their mind if you use your gift of age to make them glad that you are alive.

Some people spend time with you because they are part of your family. You may think they resent the time and effort it takes to visit you and to help you—and at times they may. The person who does well at being old helps those who offer help. Let visits with you be times of peace and quiet. Everyone needs someone to listen, so be a good listener. A thank-you and a smile will make a visitor want to return. A guilt trip or a pity party will surely keep visitors away.

For life on this earth to be worthwhile, it needs a purpose. Arvilla was right. Being a little old lady was the most difficult job of her life. Difficult jobs challenge our ability. But the difficult jobs also are opportunities to use the love God has given us through Jesus Christ.

Prayer: Thank You, Lord God, for the gift of age. Give me the gifts of the Spirit that will help me to do a good job in this stage of my life. In Jesus' name. Amen.

For Reflection

- List people you know who are older than you and who can teach you how to do your job well as an older adult. Remember, you want to become a professional old person, not just an amateur.

- List people you know who are younger than you and who might learn from your experience. Give them some on-the-job training on how to be a successful old person.

Eldon Weisheit

Keep Focused

Do you not know that in a race all the runners run, but only one gets the prize? Run in such a way as to get the prize.

1 Corinthians 9:24

The baseball team had a winning streak, then came the slump. The home-run hitters hit fly balls to the outfield, the regular pitchers seemed tired, and the infield players committed numerous errors. Finally, in a TV interview, the team's manager said, "When the players begin to focus on the game, there will be more wins." It is difficult to understand how players could lose focus. How could that happen with all the training, with division play-offs, even with the World Series at stake?

In the Bible passage, St. Paul used a sports event of his day to convey a message. If the runner is not focused on the goal, he will not enter the winner's circle to receive the champion's wreath. That wreath was important, but it would not last forever. St. Paul wrote of the lasting prize that God will graciously give when the race of this life ends.

As a believer in our Savior Jesus Christ, we too keep our eyes focused on the goal of everlasting life. We are winners! Christ's never-ending relationship with us surpasses the value of all earthly prizes. The real calling we have in our daily lives is to "declare the praises of Him who called you out of darkness into His wonderful light" (1 Peter 2:9). This "light" is our new life, and by the power of the Holy Spirit, we want to focus our lives in His direction.

Each cycle of life has hazards that distract us and may cause us to lose focus. Perhaps you can recall such events in your life. What was it that helped you refocus? Was it remembering a Bible passage or receiving encouragement from a Christian friend? Some have used the sign of the cross to remind them of their Baptism and adoption into God's family. Others will ask "Whose am I? Why am I here? Where am I going?" to remind themselves that they are God's people and called to be His witnesses. All these can help us focus on Christ and His purpose for us.

As we reach milestones in life, we have unique opportunities to demonstrate our focus. Masses of people experience retirement and longevity. God has placed us in this particular time to use the tools of our age and social changes to share spiritual goals with others.

How can we best respond to our God-given opportunities? Spend a few minutes thinking about your answer, then share it with a friend. With this challenge in mind, keep focused on all that the heavenly Father has done for you through the life, death, and resurrection of Jesus Christ. By the power of the Holy Spirit, consider how you can respond to the challenges of a new day. "This is the day the LORD has made; let us rejoice and be glad in it" (Psalm 118:24).

Prayer Suggestion: Ask the Lord for additional opportunities to share your faith.

For Reflection

- Was there a time when you lost the true focus of your life? What restored your focus?
- How can we encourage one another to stay focused?
- How could the retirement years become a special time to express our faith?

Roy Brockopp

Heads I Win,
Tails I Win

I was sitting in the backyard while Dave, who is in third grade and lives next door, and some of his friends were playing baseball. Dave and a friend began to argue about who would bat first. Each insisted it was his turn. Finally, another boy said, "Why don't you two just flip for it?" Dave immediately dug into his pocket, pulled out a coin, and said, "Okay, heads I win, tails you lose." It was an expression I hadn't heard since my childhood. Dave wanted to be a sure winner.

The apostle Paul saw himself as a sure winner—a "heads I win, tails I win" child of God. In Romans 8:28 he writes, "In all things God works for the good of those who love Him." Not *some* things, not *many* things, not *most* things, but *all* things. Paul certainly suffered at times. He craved relief and probably felt like a loser. In describing his affliction, he wrote, "Three times I pleaded with the Lord to take it away from me" (2 Corinthians 12:8). But after the Lord said Paul was already a winner,

Paul wrote in that same chapter, "When I am weak, then I am strong" (verse 10). In Philippians 1:21, Paul even wrote, "For to me, to live is Christ and to die is gain." Heads I win, tails I win. What a message! What a message to share with our children, grandchildren, and friends.

As we reflect on our lives, we see how God's grace has been sufficient. We realize how we have been, still are, and will be winners. As we look back, we also remember times when we felt and acted like losers—times when we couldn't understand why we received no relief from our problems. We struggled like losers until we joined Paul in looking to our Lord, trusting His promises and realizing that we are winners.

We are winners first because of what God has done. Long before our birth, God planned our rescue from sin and the devil. He chose us and fulfilled His plan of salvation. If people ask us what they need to do to be saved, we can only say, "Sorry, but you can't do anything. God has done it all in Christ." Heads we win, tails we win because of what God did long before we were born.

Second, we're winners because of what God is doing. The Holy Spirit works in us the faith that accepts redemption. If we want to have a "heads I win, tails I win" philosophy, we rely completely on Jesus.

While we know that we can depend on the Savior, our temptation is to hold back, harbor pet sins, obey our sinful flesh, and keep our worries. When we don't rely totally on God, we feel like losers. We are losers! We also feel like losers when we turn our attention inward. We worry about our faith, especially as we become older. We think "I don't have enough faith for this" or "My faith is too weak to handle this problem."

If we came to a bridge and didn't know if it was strong enough to hold us, would we sit down and examine our faith? Would we say, "I don't know if I have enough faith"? Would we turn our attention inward? No, we would examine the bridge. Applying this idea to our lives, we don't examine our faith; we examine God's promises. We see others resting on God. The Holy Spirit gives us the faith to say and to believe, "Heads I win, tails I win!" Real joy is ours because God promises to be with us and to work in all things for our good.

Finally, we're winners because of what God will do for us. "To die is gain," Paul writes. Heads we win, tails we win because God has prepared a place for our eternal joy. God's guarantee for our future has implications for the time we spend on earth. As we grow older, our many experiences can help us realize that we need not worry about the little things we want. God has given us the big things. He even gave His Son. There's no chance involved; all matters are in His hands. This is the message we can share with all people.

Being winners doesn't mean that we take an "I don't care" attitude toward life. It does mean that we humbly submit ourselves to God because of what He has done, what He is doing, and what He will do for us. In this knowledge our lives are filled with Christian joy.

It isn't always easy to maintain a "Heads I win,

tails I win" philosophy and to humbly submit to our Lord. But God is not just an observer in our lives. He's an active participant who guides, pushes, leads, helps, and blesses us to live as full-time winners. This is a message we can share with others who feel no joy in their lives or who feel like losers.

Prayer Suggestion: Think of someone who is hurting or who feels like a loser. Ask God to equip you to listen and witness to that person.

For Reflection

- Arrange to spend some time with the person for whom you prayed. Let God lead you as you listen, show your care, and as you share.

- When do you most feel like a loser? Of what can you remind yourself to change that feeling? What difference will feeling like a winner make in what you think, say, and do?

Les Bayer

He Knows What He's Doing— Do You?

He asked this only to test him, for He [Jesus] already had in mind what He was going to do.

John 6:6

I delight in the stories about Jesus found in the gospel of John. At first, the message seems simple and straightforward, but after further study, I find them loaded with intriguing bits and fascinating pieces. Read the story of the time Jesus fed the 5,000 (see John 6:1–15).

Take the boy, for example. What if, instead of a boy, it was a grown man who carried the loaves and fish? Judging by what I hear today, the 5,000 would have gone home hungry. This man's modern response to sharing with others might sound like this: "Wait a minute. Those are my fish. I caught them. I cleaned them. I smoked them and brought them. Now *I'm* going to eat them. I won't pamper people who don't plan. Let them take care of themselves! Sorry. But, Jesus, would You like a roll?"

The little boy didn't say that. He spoke with actions and handed over his lunch. Five thousand ate heartily. Does this incident have application for today?

Now read verse 13. Perhaps Jesus grinned from ear to ear when He asked the disciples to gather the leftovers. These were the same disciples who couldn't come up with an answer when He asked, "Where shall we buy bread for these people to eat?" (John 6:5). They could hardly believe the question had been asked! As the sun set, they stood with 12 baskets of leftovers—one for each disciple who thought it couldn't be done.

Next, take the little teaser, "Have the people sit down" (John 6:10). I've spent a career urging people to sit down and start things on time. That's not easy to do! I can hear echoes across the centuries, "Who put them in charge of my sitting? Why do I have to sit here? I don't want to sit with the sun in my eyes. I'm hungry. Let's beat the crowd and find something to eat."

That was quite a day when Jesus fed the multitude. It started with people who thought they had a good thing going, a kind of mobile Mayo Clinic. It ended with Jesus serving as the divine caterer.

The point of the story, however, isn't mired in the behavior of the characters. Instead, we learn that God has a plan. Verse six says, "He already had in mind what He was going to do." In other words, Jesus already knew how the crowd would eat.

You don't suppose that thought is a life pattern, do you? You don't suppose there is a God who watches out for His own, do you? I mean, you don't suppose that Psalm 91:11–13 is reliable, do you? And what about Matthew 7:7? Or Isaiah 43:25? Or any of a hundred other verses?

How you answer this core question likely will determine whether you finish this devotion or close this book right now so you can get busy doing something else. If you suspect that God has a plan and purpose for your life, I have good news. He does. God wants you to believe Jesus is the Christ, His Son, and believing this, you have life through His name. What a plan!

Prayer: Thank You, Lord, for planning my salvation. Use me to reveal those plans to people who don't know what You have done for them. In Jesus' name. Amen.

For Reflection

- By God's plan, the Holy Spirit brought you to faith. What other plans of God can you identify as your faith has been nourished throughout your life?
- Why is it good that God did the planning for your faith and salvation rather than leaving it up to you?

Charles S. Mueller Sr.

Upheld by God— in All Adversity

Adversity is a part of every human life. No matter how carefree and upbeat we might feel today, we all have lived through moments, days, and even years when we had to deal with adversity. Serious detours in our plans or nagging problems have troubled our bodies, hearts, or minds.

Why is dealing with adversity so upsetting? Most people like to maintain control over their lives—control over where and when they will go, their finances, activities in which they will participate, and where they will live.

Adversity usually removes control from our hands and puts it into the hands of others. Several examples can illustrate the point:

- You planned a trip abroad, but an illness changes everything.
- You carefully have planned your finances, but you find that the needs of a loved one are draining your resources.

- You love to read, but your eyes are going bad with no apparent hope for improvement.
- Gardening is your favorite hobby, but arthritis prevents you from bending.
- You always have been independent, but a stroke leaves you partially immobile, and you must move to a nursing facility.

A recent call from a dear friend reminded me of the suddenness with which adversity presents itself and the helpless feelings it can bring. She had been diagnosed with a form of cancer that was treatable but still serious. In one visit to the family doctor, her life became a series of tests and would soon become a series of treatments. Her voice trembled with disappointment and concern—for herself and for those she loved. But she placed herself in the arms of God, giving a beautiful testimony of her faith. As a true child of God, she knew the one way to meet adversity and overcome it.

St. Paul was a true child of God too. He faced significant problems throughout his ministry. During his lifetime, Paul was blinded, threatened, chased out of town, stoned, beaten, imprisoned, exiled, shipwrecked, and finally martyred for Christ. It is hard to conceive of one person's life span being so filled with adversity, but Paul rose above it by the power of God. Until his death, Paul responded to adversity with confidence, renewed enthusiasm to preach the Gospel, and eternal hope. Read 2 Corinthians 11:23b–29 and 2 Corinthians 4:8–11, 16–18.

Our troubles, when compared to Paul's, may pale in significance, but they still have potential to weigh heavily on us. Problems in our family, poor health, the needs of a loved one, and financial worries can depress and dishearten us.

Where did Paul find the strength and courage to carry him through his hardships? He didn't attend a stress management workshop or read a self-help book. He didn't take medication to dull the reality of his problems. Paul acknowledged that his life had ups and downs, but he revealed his source of strength in his letter to the Philippians:

> *Do not be anxious about anything, but in everything, by prayer and petition, with thanksgiving, present your requests to God. And the peace of God, which transcends all understanding, will guard your hearts and your minds in Christ Jesus. ... I know what it is to be in need, and I know what it is to have plenty. I have learned the secret of being content in any and every situation, whether well fed or hungry, whether living in plenty or in want. I can do everything through Him who gives me strength. Philippians 4:6–7; 12–13*

How we respond to adversity depends on our relationship with God. Fretting and worrying demonstrate a lack of faith in His promise that "In all things God works for the good of those who love Him" (Romans 8:28). Bitterness and complaining demonstrate our unwillingness to accept God's will. Once again, these sinful responses to problems keep us from experiencing the strength and support that God wants to provide. They deny the peace that is ours through Jesus. We need God's forgiveness for these sinful reactions to adversity. Thankfully it is always there, waiting to be received.

What a comfort it is to know that when times of adversity interrupt our lives there is always One who can help. We can turn to God in prayer and be sure of His upholding power and sustaining love. When adversity makes life seem out of control, it's time to "let go—and let God." He will restore our faith and trust and bring us true peace. With St. Paul we can learn to be "content in any and every situation," and boldly say, "I can do everything through Him who gives me strength."

Prayer Suggestion: Thank God for all the joy and blessings in your life. Then try to recall your most recent time of adversity. Recall how God carried you through it. Ask Him to let your life reflect the joy and peace you have through Him.

For Reflection

- What adversity are you experiencing now? Have you brought your concerns to the Lord (nothing is too great or too small for God to care about)? What kind of help might you expect?

- Think about the adversity of a friend or family member. How can your experience with adversity help that person?

Dorothy Schultz

Have You Blessed Anyone Lately?

The traditional role of Native American elders was to pass down ceremonies, traditions, and sacred ways. Unlike many of today's Americans, the original Americans revered age. Only after attaining many experiences would leadership or teaching be entrusted to members of the tribe.

We find similar practices in the Old Testament. Even Job's witless advisors argued, "What do you know that we do not know? What insights do you have that we do not have? The gray-haired and the aged are on our side, men even older than your father" (Job 15:9–10).

Remember the cry of several decades ago, "Don't trust anyone over 30"? We've not heard much of that lately. We are more likely to hear, "Today it isn't that people don't trust us, they just pass us by." An elderly grandmother told her grandson, who was attending the seminary, about the business of the church. She lamented that "Nobody asks us anymore."

It doesn't help for older folk to moan "Ain't it awful!" Maybe we should take another look at ourselves. What have we been doing to keep our lives, minds, and energies involved in the lives of the younger generations? How well have we kept in tune with the mission and ministries of our congregations?

It helps to go back to our Baptism. From the moment we were washed in the baptismal waters, God claimed every moment, day, year, and decade of our lives. He made us clean and suitable for His purposes. Our mission has its origins in the Garden of Eden. At the dawn of creation, God put the care and management of the universe in the hands of Adam, Eve, and their descendants. When Adam and Eve fell to Satan's temptations, God announced His salvation plan.

Despite human failures, God never gave up on His plan for salvation. With Abram, He gathered about Himself a new people. God had great hopes for them. To Abram God said, "I will make you into a great nation and I will bless you; I will make your name great, and you will be a blessing. I will bless those who bless you, and whoever curses you I will curse; and all peoples on earth will be blessed through you" (Genesis 12:2–3). This blessing reached prophetic fulfillment in the life, death, and resurrection of Jesus Christ. In Baptism, this blessing becomes the possession and the mission of every believer.

David celebrated this eternal, ongoing benediction: "Praise the LORD, O my soul, and forget not all His benefits—who forgives all your sins and heals all your diseases, who redeems your life from the pit and crowns you with love and compassion, who satisfies your desires with good things so that your youth is renewed like the eagle's" (Psalm 103:2–5).

We have the privilege of passing this blessing from generation to generation. Through our words, actions, and attitudes, the Gospel of God's grace becomes alive, active, and pervasive in the church.

Poet laureate Robert Bly claims a Norwegian Lutheran heritage. In his "Gatherings of Men," Bly helps men talk about their place, their role, and their responsibilities toward families. He talks of men as people who bless those younger than themselves. He emphasizes that this blessing is necessary and asks his readers whether they recently have blessed a younger man.

What Bly says of fathers and grandfathers applies equally to mothers and grandmothers. The blessing he talks about is more than cheering for your granddaughter as she plays on a Little League team. Have you blessed *anyone* lately? Have you bestowed the grace of God on anyone today? If not, maybe you've missed both an opportunity to bless and a chance to receive a warm blessing in return. You have a wealth of prayers and blessings to give away.

Look around. Whose life has been devastated by the loss of a job, and with it, the loss of joy and fulfillment? Find her. Call her. Write her a note. Tell her that you're curious about how things are going and that you will remember her in your prayers.

Do you know someone who is crushed—as King David was when confronted by his shameful misdeed—by some foolish, stupid remark uttered in a thoughtless moment? Other people may gossip and say, "Ain't it awful!" but you are the bearer of Good News. You know the love of Christ and the forgiveness that is ours through His work on the cross.

Martin Luther wrote: "We shall now return to the Gospel which offers counsel and help against sin in more than one way ... finally through the mutual conversation and consolation of the brethren."

Have you blessed anyone lately? There's still time. Why not do it right now?

Prayer: Make me a blessing to others as I have been blessed by You, dear Jesus. Give me the courage to speak words of blessings, even to those who may not welcome it. Amen.

For Reflection

- Have you wondered why we confer a blessing when someone sneezes? What other occasions for blessing others might be even more appropriate?

- Think of someone who would appreciate words of blessing. What specifically can—and will—you say?

Martin Brauer

Are You Worried about Aids?

Therefore, having been justified by faith, we have peace with God through our Lord Jesus Christ, through whom also we have access by faith into this grace in which we stand, and rejoice in hope of the glory of God. And not only that, but we also glory in tribulations, knowing that tribulation produces perseverance; and perseverance, character; and character, hope.

Romans 5:1–4 (NKJV)

Did you know that people who are 70 years old are the greatest carriers of Aids? That is Rol*aids*, hearing *aids*, and Band-*Aids*.

How do you handle the fact that your body parts don't cooperate with one another like they used to? Sometimes it seems the knee bone is no longer connected to the leg bone and the hipbone is no longer connected to the backbone—or at least they have a bad connection. What do you do when most of your get-up-and-go has got up and gone?

I haven't solved the problem parts of my body that want to retire before I do, so I will not pretend that I can solve this problem for you. I have found two extremes that I can avoid. One is wallowing in pity. The other is denying reality.

I know elderly people who refuse to hang out with people of their own generation because they are tired of listening to medical reports about digestive systems, lapsed memories, and other PMPs (Post-Midlife Pain). Some people wallow in their physical problems. They enjoy poor health because it gives them something to talk about. Sure we've got to talk about health problems, but we can do the talking with doctors and others who can help. The difference between talking about your physical difficulties and wallowing in them is simple. You can talk about your difficulty if you give others equal time to talk about theirs. You are wallowing in your problems if you try to outdo everyone else with your gory story.

The other extreme is denying reality. Some people, especially those who write commercials, pretend that growing old is a piece of cake. If you drink the right diet supplement, get a skilled plastic surgeon, keep your hair the right color, re-sod the empty spots, and wear flattering fashions, you will be free of signs of age. Those who tell you that older people can have the sex life of a 30-year-old, win at strenuous sports, and do without an afternoon nap need reality therapy. Some people can excel in certain areas, even as they pass the big birthdays of 80 and 90. Some younger people have tremendous physical limitations! It isn't reality to hold up the few who can set physical and mental endurance records in an effort to convince us that we possess similar potential.

The reality is that we must "play the hand that we have been dealt." Some people get gray hair at 30; others keep their natural color until their 60s. Some people inherited a better bone structure, heart, and memory. Is one person better than the other? Don't try to compete in your weak areas. And don't expect everyone to keep up with you where you excel. Differences were also true when we were younger. By the time we get older, we have learned to know ourselves and deal with limitations and abilities. Those who still don't understand this concept need to take a brief course in remedial maturity.

Growing old is not a competitive sport. Instead, like every other age of life, it is a team effort. I have a friend who has difficulty speaking because of a stroke. His wife has difficulty seeing. Her mother, who has lost her hearing, came to live with them. They say they are like the three monkeys: Speak-no-evil, See-no-evil, and Hear-no-evil. Because each has a physical limitation, they understand and support one another.

Discipline and commitment will keep us active. In the park where I take my morning walk, I always greet two men. One is 27. He sometimes runs 12 miles at six minutes a mile. The other is 95. He walks a mile every day. Who is the better athlete? I don't know, but I'm glad that both are doing what they can. I'm also glad when someone is willing to use a wheelchair, walker, or cane to remain active rather than surrender to physical limitations.

Old age is not for sissies. I have high regard for my parents' generation. By learning how to cope with the struggles of their earlier life, many have learned to deal with the negative side of old age. It may take them longer to do something, but they have more time. It may take them longer to remember a name or other fact, but they have many people and facts to remember.

We who believe in Jesus Christ need not wallow in or deny our physical difficulties. Check how Paul dealt with the issue. (See 2 Corinthians 4:16–5:10.) Although we are falling apart physically, we know we have a future with Christ. What we experience now is small and temporary compared to the future we have with Him. Our bodies are like tents—which is okay for now. When the tent wears out, we need not fret. Jesus will provide a new, resurrected body for us. Our new body will be free from all the marks of sin that afflict us in this life. Our faith in Christ helps us see over the horizon of death to the eternal home that He is preparing for us.

See you there.

Prayer: Lord God, give me relief from the pains that can be cured, strength to endure those that cannot be cured, and the faith to know the difference. I ask this through Jesus Christ, my Lord. Amen.

For Reflection

- What ails you? These problems will be cured when your body is made perfect in heaven. You can praise God for that hope now. How will you praise Jesus in heaven?

- What physical assets remain with you? How can you use them to serve the Lord?

Eldon Weisheit

Great-grandfather: A Surprise

We discovered great-grandfather's grave several years ago and shared this news with his 80-year-old grandson—my dad. His response? A nod. When I mentioned that an old newspaper said that more than a thousand people drove their horses and buggies to attend great-grandfather's funeral, my father snorted and said, "Impossible. Must be a misprint." He said nothing else.

When my brother casually mentioned that our great-grandfather and most of his family were not Christians, I was shocked. As a little girl, I often played with a second cousin who was not a believer. I never realized until recently that she, too, was a part of the larger family of unbelievers. This realization filled me with grief. Insights and questions flooded my consciousness:

- Maybe Dad avoided talking about great-grandfather because of family secrets.

- How did our great-grandfather feel when his son

married our Christian grandmother? Did that cause problems in the family?

- What about great-grandfather's ancestors? Were any of them believers?
- What if great-grandfather had been a Christian? What impact he could have had on other members of the family!

During a visit to Switzerland a few years ago, we saw the 16th-century baptismal font in which the ancestors of our Christian grandmother were baptized. What an exciting moment!

I often think about our ancestors who nurtured the faith of their children. What an indescribable blessing! What would have happened if our parents had not helped us grow in faith? We might have grown up not trusting Jesus Christ as Lord and Savior. We might be living without purpose and meaning. The life-changing implications are staggering.

Thanks be to God who gave us ancestors that passed on the Gospel and taught God's Word to their families. Thanks be to God for His grace that turned the hearts of our ancestors to Him in faith. Thanks be to God for surrounding us with a great cloud of witnesses, our ancestors, whose memories continue to inspire us today.

Learning more about my great-grandfather was sobering. He has gained significance in my life. He reminds me of the central purpose in life. Daily, we recognize that Christ's death and resurrection were for the world and that we are called to serve as witnesses to people of the Good News. Generations who hand down the faith are passing on life's greatest gift. Generational connections result in new lives.

Prayer: Thank You, Lord, for sending the Holy Spirit to those who have nurtured my faith in Jesus. Send me more people like that! Help me to pass along the Good News to those who come after me. Keep me as faithful to You as You are to me. Amen.

For Reflection

- The Holy Spirit brought you to faith. Whom did the Spirit send to help you grow in faith?
- Have you helped anyone grow in faith? What did you do? How can you continue to nurture the faith of others?

Shirley Bergman

Till Only One Thing Matters

Read Luke 7:11–17 and Colossians 2:13–15. Focus especially on these verses: "Jesus went to a town called Nain, and His disciples and a large crowd went along with Him. As He approached the town gate, a dead person was being carried out—the only son of his mother, and she was a widow. And a large crowd from the town was with her."

Luke 7:11–12

The account of Jesus raising the widow's son at Nain offers poignant reading and reflection. Jesus had just performed an impressive miracle—healing the centurion's servant at Capernaum. Now, 12 miles to the south—a day's journey on foot—Jesus, His disciples, and a sizable crowd of the curious approached the small village of Nain. At a humble entrance gate, a procession of villagers following a coffin met head-on with a

45

procession of life led by Jesus. They stopped at the narrow town gate. God meant for it to happen that way. Here life met death, and one had to yield to the other.

Jesus' heart went out to the woman whose son had died. After all, this was the funeral procession of a young, loved, and desperately needed man—the only son of a widow. The advancement of women had not come far in those days. Losing the only man in the house left that home without status and income. No wonder Jesus had compassion on this woman. By touching the casket, Jesus risked becoming ritually unclean. Never mind ritual. Jesus ignored such concerns. He cleansed. He healed. In the entrance to the village, life triumphed over death. The widow's son was raised. A procession of death became a procession of life.

It was a remarkable day at Nain.

Jesus still raises people from the dead. That's where you and I enter the picture. Sin has cast its shadow over our lives. We were "dead in ... transgressions and sins" (Ephesians 2:1). The Law that declares, "The soul who sins is the one who will die" (Ezekiel 18:4) has never been rescinded. "The wages of sin is death" (Romans 6:23) remains true. But we have the hope of Nain.

Life narrows down, and crisis comes. Suddenly, only one thing matters, and there, in the narrow place, stands Jesus. There was power in the word that Jesus spoke over the widow's son at Nain, power to raise him out of death for life. Jesus' words of healing and forgiveness free us from the procession of death and make us part of the procession of life.

The account in Luke 7 winds down with one simple phrase: "And Jesus gave him back to his mother" (Luke 7:15). Somewhat glorious, I should say. Back from what? From death. For what? For life, for walking in those paths that God had all along intended for him to walk.

Of course, this isn't just the story of what happened many centuries ago at Nain. It is also the story of what happens in your life and mine because of our compassionate Savior, Jesus Christ.

Prayer Suggestion: Pray for life, for spouse, two friends, your pastor, an ailing acquaintance, and someone who recently has experienced the death of a loved one.

For Reflection

- Think about your life. Tell a neighbor, friend, or family member of one way that your relationship with Jesus removed you from the procession of death and placed you in the procession of life.

- No doubt you have participated in funeral processions. Cars follow the hearse in a solemn procession to the cemetery. Knowing the story of the procession at Nain, of what might you think the next time you see a funeral procession?

Arnold Kuntz

Using Your Time

Do you remember the Teacher's words in Ecclesiastes 3:1? "There is a time for everything, and a season for every activity under heaven." The writer goes on to enumerate what we have experienced: birth and death, building and tearing down, laughter and tears, sadness and joy, the horrors of war and the relief of peace.

Yes, there is a season for every activity under heaven. There is a season to rest and relax. For many of us, that time has come; we no longer are employed on a regular basis. We can relax, take our rest, and enjoy the quiet comfort of retirement. We no longer face the problems, pressures, and anxieties of the working world.

But the Teacher has another word for us, "I know that there is nothing better for men than to be happy and do good while they live" (Ecclesiastes 3:12). The Teacher knew that true happiness comes from God. He knew, too, that the only proper response to God's gift is to share it. We have the gift of freedom by the Gospel, and we have the happiness it brings. Now that we have time to rest, relax, and reflect on God's abundant mercies, we have time to share the Gospel too.

We may be tempted to say, "I've done my share. Let

someone younger get involved." We may look at the events around us and say, "I don't know what this world is coming to! I just don't understand this modern generation." The Teacher has another word for us: "Whatever is has already been, and what will be has been before" (Ecclesiastes 3:15).

There truly is nothing new under the sun. Yes, circumstances may be different, but underlying factors remain the same. Sin is still sin. Jealousy, greed, hatred, bigotry, and violence are nothing new. They have prodded human behavior since the days of Adam and Eve. As the Teacher says, "What has been will be again, what has been done will be done again; there is nothing new under the sun" (Ecclesiastes 1:9).

In one way, that is a sad commentary on human behavior. In another way, it is an opportunity for those who are "chronologically gifted." We can share our insights because "we've been there, done that." We have opportunity to share with others the expertise and wisdom gained in the crucible of experience. Our church and the community in which we live desperately need volunteers with experience—skills such as we have to assist, to help make lives meaningful, and to confront life's issues.

There is a time and a season for everything under heaven. We have both the time and the experience to do good as long as we live. Besides that, we have the most important and unchanging information in the world. We can share our experiences with the grace and mercy of Jesus Christ with everyone we meet.

Prayer Suggestion: Ask God to open an avenue for you to share your knowledge and skill with someone who needs it. Ask Him to also open ways for you to share the Good News with those around you.

For Reflection

- What wisdom or insight has God given you through your experiences? Offer your services to your pastor or to a community agency to share your skill or knowledge.
- Are there ways that you can combine "resting and relaxing" with working for the Lord?

Fred A. Meyer

Laughing with the Lord

Why does religion often take itself so seriously while God remains so mirthful? Life is really a "holy hilarity" experience. As people of God, redeemed in Christ, we live on this "side" of the resurrection. We know how it all ends—Christ is victorious! Because of this knowledge, we can lighten up and see all of life as opportunities for laughter.

John 15:11 says it well: "I have told you this so that My joy may be in you and that your joy may be complete." Even with pain and problems and other reminders of Good Friday, you and I can celebrate that we are indeed Easter people. Christ did it! He lived, suffered, died, and rose again for us. He has completed the work of our salvation so we can celebrate each day the gift of life in Him.

God calls us to celebrate our faith and give other people permission to do so as well. I believe the people of God need to give others permission to laugh and celebrate their faith in the Lord. I'm reminded of a time when I spoke at a worship service. Afterward a serious usher came to me and said quietly, "You know, one of your stories almost made me smile." Maybe the next time he might even giggle!

Laughter is a blunt, brilliant, brave affirmation that death is not the final answer. Laughing with the Lord means keeping sight of Christ's final victory over death. We can laugh and smile because we know how it all turns out. That's the joy of living.

So what is there to laugh about in your life? For beginners, start with yourself. Learn how to laugh at yourself before someone else does. We do many silly and foolish things. Laughter allows us to enjoy our freedom in God's love and forgiveness and not to take ourselves so seriously. So what if we lock the keys in the car. So what if we're stuck in traffic. So what if we forgot to send a birthday card to our grandson. So what if we're all out of milk and bread. So what if the back seems to be going out more than we are. These are real problems, but to see these foibles in view of the cross and resurrection allows us to laugh and forgive and move on to the next day.

Laughter is the shortest distance between two people. Laughing with the Lord means that we celebrate that Christ is always with us—in the good times and the bad. To borrow someone's words: "We don't stop laughing because we grow old—we grow old because we stop laughing!"

Prayer Suggestion: Thank God for the gift of joy. Thank Him that you can smile and laugh. Ask God for a special measure of joy as you live a life of laughter with those around you.

For Reflection

- When are you most likely to be amused? Plan to laugh regularly and often. Make a daily "laughter appointment." Read cartoons in the paper. Share them with others. Hang out with people who make you laugh. Start a "humor file" to collect jokes and sayings to share with your grouchy friends.

- What have you laughed about today? Keep a list and review it before you go to bed. Happy dreams!

Rich Bimler

The Faith
of My Mother

I remember the sincere faith you have, the
kind of faith that your grandmother Lois and
your mother Eunice also had. I am sure that
you have it also.

2 Timothy 1:5 (TEV)

Jerry felt strange, perhaps even guilty, as he
unlocked the door to his mother's home. Maybe it
was his home now. His mother had died (he
glanced at his watch) 18 hours ago. Although he had
never lived in this house, it seemed like his childhood
home. The memories of his childhood and the presence
of his parents had moved with the furniture into this
house.

It was even more difficult for Jerry to enter his
mother's bedroom. For some reason, he tiptoed and
moved slowly. He had a mission. With his wife and children, he had gone to the church to plan the funeral. The
pastor had asked if there were any special hymns and
Bible readings that he wanted to hear. Jerry had
declined, but on his way home, he thought about the

question. After dropping his family at their home, he returned to this house and now stood in the bedroom where his mother and father had died.

He rarely had been in this room, but he remembered another bedroom—one that had been his parents' when he was a child. A Bible always rested beside the bed. He wanted to find it. When he clicked on the light, he instantly looked at the nightstand on his mother's side of the bed. There was a book, but not the black leather, red-bordered Bible he wanted.

Jerry opened the drawer of the nightstand: letters, pictures, church bulletins. He looked on the dresser: two magazines, a framed picture of himself as a baby, his parents' wedding picture, and pictures of his family.

"Did Mom stop reading the Bible after Dad died?" Jerry whispered.

Then he glanced back at the book on the nightstand. What had replaced the Bible? He picked it up. It was a Bible—only it was The Living Bible. What a surprise! She always had read from the King James Version. And when he was a child, she quoted verses in German, her mother's language. In the end, she had a modern Bible.

The Bible showed signs of heavy use. The spine had been taped to hold the book together. It bulged from clippings and pictures filed between the pages. On the inside front cover, Jerry saw a list of Bible chapters written in his mother's tiny script: Psalm 23, John 14, 1 Corinthians 15, 1 Thessalonians 4. He opened the book and found those chapters easily because each had a clipping inserted at the proper place. He noticed that selected verses of each passage were underlined in red. Were these messages left for him?

Jerry paged through various parts of the book. Almost every page had a verse number circled or a sentence underlined. He understood why his mother had marked certain passages of correction or encouragement. Others made no sense to him, but he realized they had held some special meaning for his mother.

Jerry looked at the items filed between the pages. Obituaries of family members and of people Jerry had never known. Poems—some clipped from magazines, others copied in his mother's handwriting. His children's school pictures. Several church bulletins with prayer requests underlined. A notice of a special meeting at church. A canceled postage stamp. A post card he had mailed from Europe.

Jerry held the book in his hand. He felt that someone had shuffled his mother's life into the pages of Scripture. How strange to think of God's Word and his mother's life all mingled together in the same book. Silently he carried the book back to church.

Prayer: Holy Spirit, thank You for mixing Your Word into my life. Help me share it with those who come after me. In Jesus' name. Amen.

For Reflection

- Do you have a favorite Bible? Why do you prefer it?

- When is the last time you read from a Bible other than your favorite? Do you think you might enjoy reading new words about a changeless topic? Ask your pastor to recommend another version. (You may not enjoy seeing your most beloved passages in new words, but you may find other passages that you enjoy more.)

Eldon Weisheit

Has God Forgotten?

Read Psalm 77

The older I get, the more I realize how much one can learn from those just taking their first steps on the scary road of life ("From the lips of children and infants ..." [Psalm 8:2]).

Our daughter shared a conversation she overheard at home. Our 3-year-old grandson was standing at the basement stairs, trying to muster enough courage to make the descent. Before taking the first step, he said, "Oh Jesus, it's awful dark down there. You'd better hold my hand."

Have you ever uttered a similar prayer? Looking back on my three score and nearly ten years, I know I have. But one joy of the "chronologically gifted" is that we can look back not only on the scary moments, but also on the happy outcomes. Often, hopeless situations end in blessing.

I think the psalmist had something like that in mind when he wrote:

> *I cried out to God for help. ... I thought about*
> *the former days, the years of long ago; ...*
> *My heart mused and my spirit inquired: ...*
> *Has His unfailing love vanished forever? ...*
> *Has God forgotten to be merciful? ...*
> *Then I thought, "To this I will appeal:*
> *the years of the right hand of the Most High."*
> *I will remember the deeds of the LORD;*
> *yes, I will remember Your miracles of long*
> *ago.*
>
> *Psalm 77:1, 5, 6, 8–11*

We've all been tempted to doubt and question. What's the solution? Where will our help and direction come from? How will we overcome? Where is the ray of sunshine signaling a better day? The cliché-ridden answers of the world aren't sufficient. You've heard them all. "Put on a happy face." "Keep your chin up and your shoulder to the wheel." "Give it your best shot." "Behind every cloud there's a silver lining." And you could probably add more. We once had a magnetic sign attached to the refrigerator that read, "One day as I sat musing sad and lonely, a voice came to me from out of the blue which said, 'Cheer up, things could be worse.' So I cheered up and sure enough, things got worse." Not much comfort or hope in advice like that.

"Has God forgotten to be merciful?" His answer is a resounding no! No, He has not forgotten. No, His promise has not failed. His answer is more than a quick no and a fatherly pat on the head. If we could be so bold as to paraphrase God's answer, it might sound something like this:

I haven't forgotten. Just look back on your life. Remember when you stood at the top of the dark stairway? I not only held your hand, I walked the stairs in front of you to make your way secure. Remember when you faced an "impossible" situation? You trusted Me, and now the problem is only a memory. Besides, you became a stronger person as you coped with problems. Remember when you did what I had forbidden or failed to do what I had commanded? I didn't push you aside or abandon you to figure your own way out of the mess. I picked up your burden and shouldered your guilt and helplessness. I laid all your iniquities on My dear Son. He says to you, "Be happy. Your sins are forgiven. I carried them all the way to the cross. And I didn't stop there. I held your hand as I took you to be buried with Me in your Baptism. Then I walked in front of you on that glorious third day so you could follow Me in newness of life. Remember?"

Don't forget your safety in Jesus when you cry out for help. Perhaps St. Paul said it best, "He who did not spare His own Son, but gave Him up for us all—how will He not also, along with Him, graciously give us all things?" (Romans 8:32).

That's the blessing of many years. We have so much on which to look back, so much to remember. Over the years, we have all stood at the dark stairs and said, "Oh, Jesus, it's awful dark down there. You'd better hold my hand." When we recall those times, we remember the deeds of the Lord. With the psalmist, we can remember the former days. We can echo his words, "You led Your people like a flock by the hand of Moses and Aaron" (Psalm 77:20).

It's in remembering God's mercy that we have the confident hope to look ahead. Our God will not stop doing what He always has done. His mercy endures forever. We can appeal to what we have seen and experienced over all our years at the right hand of the Most High. Remember? He has led you through the stormy seas and beside the still waters. In looking back on all that, we hear and trust His Word of promise, "I am with you always, to the very end of the age" (Matthew 28:20).

Prayer Suggestion: Ask God to "forgive your forgetting" and to sharpen your remembering of His powerful and merciful deeds in your life. Pray for strength to walk boldly with the God who has proved Himself through His Son.

For Reflection

- List five "amazing" acts of God in your life. Share your list with a friend or loved one.
- What "amazing" acts of God do you see in the lives of others? Thank God for showing His love to others.

August Mennicke

Parables and Miracles

God said. … And it was so.

Genesis 1:6–7

I wish you had known Joe. He helped me carry the Franklin stove into my living room 35 years ago. Our family knew his books, sang his songs, liked his laugh. He played songs about freedom and Martin Luther King on his autoharp. We were friends and roommates in the seminary. Joe experienced a miracle. God stretched his frail, sick heart into seven unexpected years of life.

This devotion is about parables and miracles and Joe.

Many years ago, a church debate asked the question, "Does God love miracles or parables the most?" It was the time for arguing which Bible stories are miracles or parables. Joe flew to a convention where debate reached a fever pitch. I knew he'd be at the podium making speeches, being hurt, asking hard questions. I stayed home and wrote a Christmas parable, "Alleluia and Angel Feathers."

Many liked the recording. "Alleluia and Angel Feathers" played throughout the country. In the story, the angels rehearse a glorious anthem. One angel, Theodore, does his own thing. He gathers angel feathers from dressing room floors and stuffs them into clouds. When heaven's Hosts of Angel Choirs visit earth to sing "Gloria" over Bethlehem, Theodore follows with clouds of feathers. The clouds open, and feathers cover the hillside, the shepherds, the inn, and the "Gloria" singers. I never told Joe that he was Theodore, the angel.

Joe died of heart disease. He had a big heart. I think it broke. Joe wrote songs about Moses, slavery, freedom, exile. They were biblical songs about Chicago, Birmingham, Montgomery, Selma, Detroit. Joe was about reality. He led a walk of 14 Stations of the Cross through poor towns, into places of oppression, to prisons, through wealth. Joe saw parables and miracles in literature, in news, in novels, on the street. I felt Joe swivel between past and future. He did not tell time as chronology, with a calendar. Joe pivoted like a prophet; he looked around and talked about Now Time.

In college religion class, I counted the miracles and parables recorded in each of the four gospels. Joe didn't see parables that way. He saw parables and miracles in the daily news. He saw stories in the spaces between lines. Joe looked around a word; the environment was the context. The Gospel was a circle of space and time, then and today connected.

Joe told stories and something happened. He asked

questions and people changed. Joe read the Bible a certain way and the people in a city block founded a radio station to make their families safe, to control their own lives. He started classes in housing projects instead of classrooms. He began big ideas and gave them away when they were growing. Then he'd begin something new for someone's future. Joe preached and people were stirred up, they acted. Joe was out ahead; we were catching up. He acted like a prophet but never said so.

I like parables—and miracles. Joe helped me like them by the way he saw things. I remember one occasion. In a Holden Village vespers, I asked two mimes to tumble and dance. Miracle dressed in white tights, Parable in black. One mirrored the other. Miracle and parable are two sides of God's love. A love miracle told right is a love parable. A love parable heard well creates a love miracle. A good story will change life. So will a good miracle. I wonder why we sometimes break one another's heart when looking at God's Word of love.

Sometimes we fight because we do not see what the other sees—we miss Theodore adoring with angel feathers. Years passed after that debate at the convention. Those who fought now sang the same songs, saw the connection between miracle and parable, believed the miracle of God in both.

Joe and I didn't talk much, but we had similar ideas. Joe helped me see more wholly. A woman asked me to buy her son a red-letter Bible. They were out of print. She was sorry. I phoned and asked, "Why are you more interested in what Jesus said than what Jesus did?" She responded, "Then get me one which prints what Jesus did in red." These are not in print. Love is about what Jesus said and does and is. Love is about what we say, and do, and are—all of these.

Joe is a true story. I liked true stories when I was little. True love stories I heard are working miracles in me. When a good thing happens, I try to tell it right so it can be spontaneous, like a parable. Then I watch what it does to the hearer.

A thousand books are in my library. Most of my footnotes are by people I know, like Joe. We are one another's *op cits* and *ibids*. People think about what we say and do. We are noted, quoted, remembered.

Today look for miracles. Think how you can describe it so others will believe by your telling.

Prayer: O God, Your Word is deed. Your truth is said and done. You spoke and it was so. You speak and there is life. Hold us close to the wonder of Your Word and of Your work. In Jesus' name we pray. Amen.

For Reflection

- What miracles has God done in your life? (Don't forget the one called "faith.")
- How can you take the words of Jesus' love and turn them into action?

Herbert Brokering

Too Old for What?

Being confident of this, that He who began a good work in you will carry it on to completion until the day of Christ Jesus.

Philippians 1:6

The other day I heard a mother say, "You are too old for that!" I don't know what it was for which her child was "too old," but it set me thinking. Is there a time when one is "too old" for something?

When Moses was about 40 years old, God told him to rescue his people from their mistreatment at the hands of the Egyptians. But Moses had problems, and he fled to the wilderness. He stayed in the wilderness for 40 years, got married, and became a shepherd. He lived as a nomadic herdsman, probably a mostly peaceful life. Then the angel of the Lord called to him from the burning bush, called him to be the leader that God intended him to be.

Now Moses was older and less self-confident. He questioned the Lord's judgment, making many excuses, most of which came from the humility he had learned in the wilderness. Certainly there must be something wrong with the Lord's timetable! An 80-year-old man called into service?

Moses debated God's call, but not on the basis of his age! Despite his misgivings, Moses obeyed God's call and served his Lord with vigor.

Like Moses, Joshua was about 80 years old when God called him to lead Israel into the Promised Land. (See the first six chapters of Joshua.) Instead of a younger man, God chose someone who might be called "over the hill" or "long in the tooth" to lead Israel. Joshua might have questioned God's wisdom. He might have asked, "Why me? Why not choose someone younger, more vigorous, more popular?" He might have reasoned that he was "too old" for this sort of thing. But Scripture makes no mention of any hesitancy on Joshua's part. He trusted God and confidently assumed leadership of the children of Israel.

You may remember how the story ended. God gave Joshua outstanding success. Town after town, city after city, fell before the advancing Israelite nation. The Promised Land was theirs, just as God had promised.

The narratives of Moses' and Joshua's leadership in Israel pose an intriguing thought for those of us who are "chronologically gifted." Is there such a thing as being "too old" to accept a challenge? Is there a time when experience or training are obsolete?

We received our call from the Lord at our Baptism. We have observed our Lord's hand at work in our lives. We have had many experiences, and we have God-given gifts. Who knows what our Lord has in store for us, what opportunities for service He will place before us? One thing we do know: Our gracious Lord has seen us through to this time in our lives; He will continue to provide the same loving care He showered on us in the past.

The Lord, who gives older adults strength, will also give us the ability to serve Him in many ways. When He provides a new challenge, He promises to be our shepherd and our guide. We can, like Moses and Joshua, confidently accept His opportunities for service. We can be His instruments, bringing the Good News of Jesus Christ to others, speaking encouragement to those who need uplifting. We can follow the footsteps of Moses and Joshua, those older adults whom God called into His service.

Prayer Suggestion: Think for a moment about the times God guided you. Give Him thanks for His tender care. Ask Him to open your eyes to new challenges.

For Reflection

- In which experiences do you feel most confident? Look for an opportunity to use your experiences to help someone.
- Is there such a thing as being "too old" to accept a challenge? Which challenges are reasonable? Which are unreasonable?

Fred A. Meyer

I Go to Parties

And whether one member suffer, all the members suffer with it; or one member be honored, all the members rejoice with it.

1 Corinthians 12:26 (KJV)

I go to parties—to the golden anniversary celebration for a couple. Many people attended the party, including some whose spouse had died after 47, 39, or 32 years of marriage. I see others who were divorced after 25 or 30 years of marriage. Still others were never married. We're all at the party, and we all rejoice with the couple celebrating their 50th anniversary.

I go to parties—to the retirement party for a person who completed a successful career. I listen to speeches that honor him for his great accomplishments. I see the gifts he receives. I look around me. Some people were laid off from the career they loved before they could retire. When they do retire, it's from a job they took only to wait out the years. Some worked all their lives at a place that did not offer a retirement party. Others worked for themselves and received only their own thanks. But we all were there to celebrate a retirement.

I go to parties—to the party after a funeral. I see a family together. I hear the deceased's children, grandchildren, and great-grandchildren honor and respect the one who died. I hear them express appreciation and love. Listening to those same speeches are others who had no children, those whose children have died, and others whose children give no honor or respect. We all are there to share the happiness of a family that loved one another and loved us.

I go to parties—to a housewarming for a new home. I see the beautiful house filled with a lifetime of collected treasures. I see the souvenirs the family brought back from faraway countries. I see their trophies and awards. I see other guests who live in simple, furnished apartments. I see others who must live with extended family. We are all there to celebrate the joy of a new home.

I go to parties where healthy people bask in their energy and others come in wheelchairs or with oxygen tanks. I go to parties and think of those who are never invited anywhere—and who never invite others to a party.

I tell you about these parties because I want you to think about the times you are with other people. Where did you see yourself at each of the parties I described? Were you the one who had everything and invited others to share your joy? Were you the one with little who was expected to be happy for others?

Sometimes I'm the one filled with joy at parties. Sometimes I'm the one who must be content with the secondhand joy of others. I've learned to enjoy all the parties because I have noticed something. Jesus attends the same parties. He's there because He loves me; He goes along with me. I am fortunate that most of the people whose parties I attend also believe in Jesus. He is their guest too. I always enjoy a meal more when we can say together, "Come, Lord Jesus, be our guest."

When I am the one with visible blessings at a party, I am glad that Jesus is there. He reminds me that my honor does not come from great achievements or accomplishments. He gave me His grace. What I have came from His blessings. Whatever joy I have, I want to share with others. I rejoice that those who don't have the same blessing can rejoice for me.

When I see others rejoice over blessings that I don't have, I am glad that Jesus is there too. He takes away the jealousy and the judgment that is part of my sinful nature. He helps me rejoice that someone else shares their blessing with me.

Could you think of reading or hearing this book as a party we are attending together? I like to think of it that way. I'd like to hear about the things that make you happy so I can share in that happiness. I'd like to hear about the things that cause your heart to ache so I can take some of that pain for a moment. We can be together that way because Jesus is with you and He is with me. When you look at a party that way, you realize that people who are far away can be near to you through love.

Prayer:

We have come, Lord Jesus,
We are your guests.
Let your gifts
To us be blessed. Amen.

For Reflection

- What do you remember about the last party you attended? Was Jesus there? How could you tell?
- How can it be true that though you are separated by miles, you can still feel close to loved ones?

Eldon Weisheit

Relax in His Love

A magazine article reported a story about the construction of a tall building. The framework and skeleton were finished, however, the work was running far behind schedule. Some people worked nights to catch up.

One man, working in the dark, remembered that he left a toolbox high in the framework. He rode the work elevator to retrieve it. As he walked along one of the beams, he tripped. As he slipped, however, he managed to grab the beam and hang there.

The worker struggled and pulled and tried to get his legs back up, but didn't have the right grip or the strength to succeed. He screamed and hollered, but noise from machinery prevented anyone from hearing. He pulled with all his strength but couldn't get up. His hands began to ache. Finally, his fingers became numb. With a shriek of horror, he let go. As he reported later, he probably fell about 10 inches—onto a wooden scaffold that some workers had used during the day.

Our problem situations are frequently like that of the worker, at least in our response. In times of trouble, we often struggle, kick, scream, and try to help ourselves through our own power. When our efforts fail, we fear the worst. However, when we turn to God, He is there to catch and hold us. When we look back in our lives, we can recall situations when we struggled with a problem instead of relaxing in God's love. There are some big differences between our situations and that of the workman. I'd like to mention a few.

First, the man didn't know the scaffold was beneath him. Children of God have experienced His help in the past and know that God is there to catch, save, bless, and help. Still, we struggle and kick, even when we can't do anything about the situation. We struggle rather than trust God.

Second, God isn't there only to catch us. He actually reaches out to hold us and love us. He's there to calm our fears no matter what the fears might be—even fears of death. God already has gone all the way for us. He gave His only Son to live, suffer, and die for us. If He loved us that much, He's certainly going to keep us in His care.

Third, God doesn't reach out in His love and simply wait for us to collapse. He is more than a patient spectator. He's in the struggle with us. He's guiding and leading us. He's brought us to faith and keeps us in faith. He's blessing us and helping us remember His blessings of the past. He helps us love others. He's there to help us be role models, especially for His younger children. Absolutely nothing can separate us from His love. There's nothing powerful enough to take us away from God. Even death is conquered because Jesus overcame it.

Several verses in Romans 8 speak of these differences between our situation and that of the worker hanging on the beam.

We know that in all things God works for the good of those who love Him, who have been called according to His purpose. ... If God is for us, who can be against us? He who did not spare His own Son, but gave Him up for us all—how will He not also, along with Him, graciously give us all things? Who will bring any charge against those whom God has chosen? It is God who justifies. Who is he that condemns? Christ Jesus, who died— more than that, who was raised to life—is at the right hand of God and is also interceding for us. Who shall separate us from the love of Christ? Shall trouble or hardship or persecution or famine or nakedness or danger or sword? ... No, in all these things we are more than conquerors through Him who loved us. For I am convinced that neither death nor life, neither angels nor demons, neither the present nor the future, nor any powers, neither height nor depth, nor anything else in all creation, will be able to separate us from the love of God that is in Christ Jesus our Lord. Romans 8:28, 31–35, 37–39

May God help us relax in His love. May He touch our lives with love and blessing. May the Holy Spirit increase our faith and enable us to serve God and His people.

Prayer Suggestion: Speak a prayer of thanks for a specific gift from God and for all the times the Lord reached out to rescue you.

For Reflection

- Talk with your spouse or close friends about how God has been active in your life. Ask them to share experiences as well.
- Were God's blessings ever a surprise? Did He help you even when you didn't ask for help? What does that tell you about God?

Les Bayer

To Life

Read Psalm 1.

Life is precious to all of us. We marvel at the birth of a child and rejoice with the family of the new-born. Many of us shudder at the thought of our own death. We observe people living day by day, pushing the thought of death from their mind, trying to find the "good life" in the here and now.

Dying is the ultimate earthly experience of faith. It's as if in our dying hour, we stand in faith before our Father and say: "This is it. I claim the heaven You promised not because of my merits but because of the life, death, and resurrection of Your Son." That claim isn't pronounced out of disrespect or defiance. We speak the words in childlike boldness and confidence, in humility and awe, before the almighty God who has shown such great love for His wayward children.

Our claim on heaven is based on God's promises. In John 11 the Son of God said: "I am the resurrection and the life. He who believes in Me will live, even though he dies; and whoever lives and believes in Me will never die" (John 11:25–26). This statement about the future of the faithful is clear and plain. Those who believe in Christ will live forever in heaven with the Savior. He died for all sinners, rose from the dead, and returned to His heavenly Father to prepare a place for us.

Jesus also had words for our earthly life. He said, "I have come that they may have life, and have it to the full" (John 10:10). He wants us to be content with life—to enjoy it fully. When life becomes frail and difficult, Jesus wants us to remember the part of life still living fully within us, immune to suffering, sickness, and even death.

The full life begins with the gift of faith. We live fully in God's grace, not with the specter of death hovering over us. Before we were children of God, we lived outside God's family. We were not His children. We were His enemies. We were destined for eternal punishment. But Jesus made us right with God through His life, death, and resurrection. We now live in our heavenly Father's forgiving love. We are free to serve Him, free to live out the full life!

Obstacles to living the full life can slow us down. "Why this catastrophe?" "Why that untimely death?" "What does the future hold for my family and me?"

The gentle words of Jesus quiet our souls when we read: "Peace I leave with you; My peace I give you. I do not give to you as the world gives. Do not let your hearts be troubled and do not be afraid" (John 14:27). When agents of darkness unsettle us, or events in life plant doubts about God's love, Jesus reminds us of the peace that He brings. We need not fear. He controls all things, even those situations that trouble us. As our faith matures, we rely on Christ, the Rock on which we build our life, the Fortress that gives us safe haven in troubled times.

How does one describe the "full life"? It's a combination of the sacred and secular in the life experiences of Christians. These experiences may include the sweet memories of God's forgiveness after a bitter bout with sin; the trust exhibited when bringing a child to the baptismal font; the long-awaited reconciliation with a loved one; the joy of people together in worship and praise; the anguish over a child who has wandered from faith; thanksgiving for God's reclaiming a lost one; God's comfort at the death of a loved one. Still more may be gratitude to God for a new home, a new car, a new coat, or a sandwich; a look at the sunset; success in a new endeavor; the joy of discovery in God's world; a new scriptural insight; a cake recipe that everyone liked. The list could be longer than this book.

Prayer: Dear Father in heaven, You are the giver of all life. Thank You for Your kept promises. Thank You for the promise of eternal life. Please keep me aware of Your presence and of Your many blessings. I pray in the name of Your Son, my Brother and Savior. Amen.

For Reflection

- What would you add to the thanksgiving list in the last paragraph of the devotion?

- Which blessings can you share with others? What blessings are others willing to share with you? When you share your blessings, do you expect anything in return? What do you always receive in return?

Ed Krueger

Called to Serve

God called Paul to serve in a dramatic way. Paul's life was literally turned around when God chose him to begin the first foreign missions. Read about this event in Acts 9:1–22.

Few of us have experienced God's call as sensationally as St. Paul did, but we, too, were called to serve our Lord Jesus. When did it happen to you? How did you know what God was calling you to do? Whom did God use to help you realize your calling?

Your first call to serve came at Baptism. Through the water and the Word, the Holy Spirit made you a member of God's family. Perhaps you were called again through a lesson, clearly taught by a Sunday school teacher, or through a sermon that touched your heart. Or did someone tap you on the shoulder—a parent, relative, teacher, or pastor—and say that you were the kind of person whose gifts and talents God could use? Was it a still, small voice inside that reminded you of Jesus' directive to go and make disciples that brought you to serve Him? Sometimes God puts roadblocks where He does not want us to go. Sometimes He puts us in just the right place at the right time to become a part of a special ministry to family, community, or congregation.

Many Christians who are "chronologically gifted" have spent their lives in service to others—at home, at their job, and in volunteer work for the church and community. Their lives have been both filled and fulfilled. Sometimes retirement is viewed as a time to *stop* doing anything that resembles work—or serving others. It's viewed as a time to start serving self. This can be accomplished by spending countless hours on the golf course, reading, or traveling. While we can value a less-demanding lifestyle, God calls us to serve Him all of our lives—which gives us a purpose for living. The precious gift of unscheduled time is available now, not only to use and enjoy, but also to share with others!

Consider seriously the talents and gifts that God gave you and the many experiences you have had that make life rich and full. What do you see as your strengths? Are you a good listener, an effective leader, a handy helper, a teacher, a good grandparent, a handi-crafter, an encourager, an organizer, a gardener, a Bible student, a cook, a good shopper, a person of prayer? God provides these gifts, uniquely yours, and He asks you to serve Him by helping others.

As you recognize your gifts, identify who might benefit from them. Perhaps you are actively using your talents to serve others. But if you are a senior who finds time dragging slowly—or if you're increasingly self-absorbed, bitter, anxious, and losing your sense of purpose—it's time to regroup. Consider how you might make a difference in the life of a neighbor, relative, or church member. It's time to ask God to renew your heart and mind as you dust off your call to serve.

Good listeners have a unique calling. Loving listeners help people with problems by allowing them to share their burdens with one who cares. Shut-ins would surely enjoy a visit from you, or they might appreciate a specially baked treat from an ambitious baker or flowers from a home gardener. You might be the one who can shop for groceries or other needs. The love you bring and share reflects the love of Jesus and will truly warm the heart of one of His own.

Handy helpers can provide simple repairs to church facilities or for people in the community who are unable to make them or pay for them. A good organizer can orchestrate food donations to families in crisis— when serious illness or sudden death intrudes on life. Teachers can tutor underprivileged children. Loving grandparents can read stories and volunteer at children's centers. Bible students can organize home Bible studies. Handicrafters can teach their skills to others who also could enjoy creating things of beauty. Encouragers are welcome everywhere, especially in hospitals and nursing homes. Effective leaders are needed as volunteers and consultants in many areas of church management. And persons of prayer are always ready to take their burdens, and those of others, to the Lord, laying them at His feet and seeking His guidance.

God said of St. Paul, "This man is My chosen instrument to carry My name before the Gentiles and their kings and before the people of Israel" (Acts 9:15). Paul listened to the Lord and fearlessly followed Him. God says the same to us, and we follow Him when we look beyond ourselves to the needs of others, seeking to share His love and His Word. As we listen to the Lord, we too recognize that He calls us to serve Him—even in retirement. How will God use you today? This week? For the remainder of this year? What exciting challenges does He have for you? As one of God's people, called to serve, you will see in the needs of others blessed opportunities to answer His call. May God grant it!

Prayer Suggestion: If you have let your call to serve lapse, seek God's forgiveness. Ask Him to renew you through the power of the Holy Spirit so you might become aware of those who can benefit from your unique talents and gifts.

For Reflection

- Name one person or one cause that you can help by praying. Then seek God's will to discover what is needed and how you can serve.

- As you pray to help others, could you be the answer to your own prayer? How might God use you to help?

Dorothy Schultz

Darkness and Light

You may remember the story of a little girl named Virginia who doubted the existence of Santa Claus. Though her father assured her that Santa Claus existed, she nevertheless felt unsettled and wrote a letter to a newspaper asking, in her childlike way, "Is there really a Santa Claus?"

The editor of the paper, smitten with the sweet naiveté of the question, replied in a famous editorial that won widespread fame, "Yes, Virginia, there is a Santa Claus."

Unknown to most, Virginia remained unsatisfied and decided to write directly to the source. Her letter begged, "Dear Santa Claus, do you really exist?"

In his reply, Santa said, "Dear Virginia, I note that your academic proficiency does not include a grasp of existentialism. Therefore, instead of toys and other goodies, I will give you books by such authors as Kierkegaard, Comte, and Sartre."

Asking difficult questions can be hazardous. Yet we continue to ask them. "God, do You really exist? If You really exist, why do You allow so much pain in the world? Specifically, why did You allow that 6-year-old child to be gunned down in a drive-by shooting? More specifically, why did You allow my bright and vivacious daughter to die of cancer before she was 20?"

Do you have questions you would like to add?

Questions such as these reveal a certain darkness of the soul that afflicts all of us from time to time. Doubt brings such darkness whether or not we like it. Perhaps this is because we have learned to be more comfortable with clear-cut answers than with ambiguity.

But the Lord does not always communicate on our wavelength. You may recall that Jesus' disciples often were frustrated by His parables. One time after He explained a parable, they thanked Him for "finally" speaking plainly!

We, too, are grateful for the things Jesus makes clear: He is the way of salvation. We are saved by faith, not works. Faith without works is dead. Paul says, "My purpose is that they may be encouraged in heart and united in love, so that they may have the full riches of complete understanding, in order that they may know the mystery of God, namely, Christ" (Colossians 2:2). But many other aspects of faith life are conveyed indirectly. Why does the Lord do this? That's a question worth pondering.

Perhaps one reason is that the very distress caused by such ambiguity increases our dependence on God and His promises rather than on our own wisdom and rational powers. The mystery of the sacraments, Baptism and the Lord's Supper, underline His wisdom because by their nature, mystery and ambiguity are closely related.

God and His good will are not a matter of knowing in the usual sense that we come to know about other things. He does not allow us the luxury of "nailing Him down." God cannot be put in His place once for all like dates in history, formulas from chemistry, or the like. In a way, He says, "Don't put Me on the level of the totally knowable."

In our relationship to our Lord, we often are preoccupied with closing a credibility gap rather than seizing His promises and holding on for dear life. We often prefer to talk our faith rather than act it out. We feel comfortable when we have an adequate arsenal of words with which to take on all comers who want God explained. Thereby, we rob God of His proper mystery, of His "not yet."

As we live out our life on earth, we may need to "unlearn" some lessons of life. One of the most stubborn, perhaps because it was learned at a great price, is that of self-sufficiency. Simply put, we have learned to depend on ourselves for solving many of life's problems. In the material world, we may take great pride in having achieved a lovely home, late-model car, and well-educated children.

Later in life, self-sufficiency becomes of less value in the array of important questions to be asked and answered, especially as we realize that we are not equipped with adequate answers. Our self-sufficiency then needs to be converted even more to God's sufficiency, which is sufficient for all our needs.

Prayer Suggestion: Thank God for the questions He has allowed you to answer. Praise Him for additional confidence in His all-sufficiency.

For Reflection

- What questions have bothered you that you have not been able to answer? Don't be afraid to confront them. Make a list of them under the title: "These are the things I want to ask God when we meet face to face." The list will offer both relief and a sense of satisfaction ... but not self-sufficiency! Make another list, similar to the list above, under the heading: "Blessings for which I want to thank God."
- Read Isaiah 60:1–6.

Wayne Lucht

Your Flight Is Now Boarding

Simeon took [Jesus] in his arms and praised God, saying: "Sovereign Lord, as You have promised, You now dismiss Your servant in peace. For my eyes have seen Your salvation, which You have prepared in the sight of all people, a light for revelation to the Gentiles and for glory to Your people Israel."

Luke 2:28–32

You would not expect to see many signs of the church at 2 A.M. in an airport. You would look in vain for a cross. Occasionally, you might find a little chapel, as at Lambert International Airport in St. Louis, Mo.—you might even see a pastor in attendance. He might be listening to the troubled sobbing of a young mother with two young children in tow. He might hear a distraught traveler's confession, seeking absolution. He might hear a prayer.

More significant, you might join the simple liturgy

in progress with two or three other travelers. The liturgy would include praying the Lord's Prayer, speaking the Apostles' Creed, and listening to a favorite Scripture passage. Quietly, it will dawn on you that among hundreds of weary travelers, you are in the midst of God's holy Christian Church. Having never met or seen a single member of this gathering, the truth of Jesus' words dawn on you: "Where two or three come together in My name, there am I with them" (Matthew 18:20). You are strangely aware of the presence of Jesus Christ.

A great hymn of Christmas says it well.

> *Oh, rejoice all Christians, loudly,*
> *For our joys have now begun:*
> *Christ is born as Mary's Son.*
> *Tell abroad his goodness proudly,*
> *Who our race has honored so,*
> *That he lives with us below.*

Abruptly you are roused from your meditation by a harsh voice barking, "Flight 203 to San Diego is now boarding." In the hurry to get to the gate, your thoughts of reverent devotion disappear. You are more concerned with boarding the plane with all your luggage and hoping that your boarding pass is in good order.

When we read about Simeon in the gospel of Luke, we get the idea that he was a bearded old man, ready and waiting to die. That's what we understood from older translations that read, "Now let Your servant depart in peace." Newer translations have Simeon saying,

"You now dismiss Your servant in peace" (Luke 2:29), as if Simeon might have been on assignment, perhaps temple duty, and having completed his work, he is ready to move on to other tasks. While accepting the fact that his death was now nearer than ever before and that he was quite ready for it, Simeon might have been thinking about his future on earth as well.

For you and me, it would be helpful to think of this benediction in terms of our next task. Seventy, 80, or 90 years old, the Lord has not summoned us home. There is still much for us to do. We're still busy being aunts and uncles, sisters and brothers, and, of course, grandparents and maybe even great-grandparents. Simeon may have returned home to be a husband and father and to take care of his vineyard and animals.

Having seen Jesus present in the wine and bread of Holy Communion, we too are dismissed to go home and do what we must do as spouses, parents, grandparents, neighbors, sisters, and brothers in the faith. We're refreshed, renewed, ready to go on with our lives as we live them under many conditions and circumstances.

While we don't know Simeon's perspective on aging and death, we are aware of our own thoughts on departing this life. In reading this simple devotion and song of Simeon, we justifiably focus our attention on our departure to be with Jesus and our Father in heaven. It's neither morose nor morbid to talk about dying. "We all have to go sometime," we say to one another. And it may be soon. As travelers in this world, we know that our time of departure is nearer than it's ever been. We do not gloomily mull over this fact, dropping our spirits into a pit of despair. In Baptism, Jesus gave us our boarding pass. Because of this, we can say simply, "Whatever You say, Lord. I'm ready. In fact, I am waiting expectantly."

Meanwhile, there is some living to do. There are blessings to bestow on a friend, neighbor, or child. No matter what comes or when it comes, everything is in order. Let the flight ascend any time.

Prayer Suggestion: You might include in your prayers those troubled by illness, family problems, loss of job—distress of any kind. Pray that they will be alert and ready for their trip to heaven.

For Reflection

- What will you say next time you hear, "We all have to go sometime"?
- What will you do with your life as you await your own departure?

Martin Brauer

It's Not over Yet

And Jesus grew in wisdom and stature, and in favor with God and men.

Luke 2:52

It's such a little word in Greek: *prokopto*. Tucked away in the last verse of the only story from Jesus' growing-up years, you could easily miss it. The Bibles I checked translate it either as *grow* or *increase*. Not bad choices. But had those translators been more attuned to human development, they might have chosen other words to make the meaning of *prokopto* more clear.

The larger story in which the word appears begins with Mary, Joseph, and Jesus enjoying an annual family event: the celebration of Passover at the temple in Jerusalem (Luke 2:41). Mary and Joseph left the city, and on the way home, their world collapsed. Remember? Miscommunication. Separation. The frantic three-day search.

It all worked out. Mom and dad found Jesus, and together, they went home. Peace came to the family's home the way it does to most: the teenage Jesus obeyed His parents. There's nothing like doing what you're told to relax tension at home!

And with that *prokopto* shows up.

Prokopto means "beat into shape" or "hack forward." It's the task of the jeweler who pounds chunks of gold into delicate shapes, or it's what the smithy does when he heats and beats iron bars into horseshoes. It's what pioneers did, axing a path through the wilderness. It's hard, slow work.

Prokopto describes the teenage years. The road from 13 to 20 is not easy. Each day brings something new, demanding, often scary. Those are tough years. But *prokopto* does not disappear at 20. It accompanies us from 20 to 30, from 40 to 50, from 70 to 80!

Many have *prokopto*-ed through those first years of marriage with the babies and diapers and not nearly enough money. A decade later, in our 30s, we were *prokopto*-ing again, pressured by a budding job that almost sapped the life from marriage, the joy from family, and the fun from friendships. "Not enough time" was our mantra!

The 40s taught that there actually is a "hill" and that you have crested it in some areas of life. Downhill looks dangerous! The 50s force you to think of the golden years to come. The 60s trot you into a hundred doctors' offices to treat complaints you never had before. And it doesn't stop there. We *prokopto* into the 70s, the 80s, the 90s, and perhaps even the 100s. Each decade is full of new issues—and the same kind of struggle.

Prokopto is part of life. Under *prokopto,* we learn to live with loss, deal with disappointment, and develop skills we don't want. Challenges flood in day by day. We wrestle with daily remolding, weekly change, monthly switches. *Prokopto* never ends. That's the way life is for us. The teens are but a foretaste, a training camp for learning how to work through re-forming experiences.

But *prokopto* isn't all downhill. Every slash of the thicket has the potential for opening new vistas, and every thump of life's sledgehammer offers new and exciting reshaping. *Prokopto* isn't something to endure reluctantly. It's what God uses to unfold life's magnificence and bring the savor of excitement to our days.

Prayer: Lord, keep my energy up and my curiosity bright so I can check out the new things You've imbedded in each day. Remind me each day that I may be older, but I'm not done yet. In Jesus' name. Amen.

For Reflection

- Want some fun? List what's new in your life this decade.
- Not much on the first list? Start another list of what could be new if you would nose around and show some of the courage you've been developing by *prokopto*-ing all these years.

Charles S. Mueller Sr.

4 × 1 = 5

And Jesus grew in wisdom and stature, and
in favor with God and men.

Luke 2:52

*P*rokopto isn't the only eye-opening idea God's
Spirit packed into the last verse of Luke 2. He
zooms in on four separate *prokopto* areas that
demanded Jesus' best effort—and ours. Can you identify
those areas? The four haven't changed in 2,000 years.

The first *prokopto* area is wisdom: intellectual
growth, the three *R*s, education. Has it been your experience that no matter what you call this *prokopto,* it
doesn't happen without effort? A lot of commitment and
midnight oil is involved in becoming smarter. Some people can sponge up knowledge faster than others. But no
matter, intellectual growth requires effort and focused
determination.

The second area Luke mentions is stature. Most
folks call it physical growth, a product of exercise,
healthy habits, good diet, the right amount of sleep. To
the young, good health comes naturally. Bulging muscles and comely curves just happen. On the other side

of 30, it's a different matter, as all the health clubs, spas, diets, and exercise classes testify. *Stature* is spelled *h-a-r-d-w-o-r-k*.

The third field in Jesus' flowering process is spiritual growth. What the Holy Spirit started (and still starts) with baby prayers and baby Bible verses and baby theological thoughts needs to bloom. It often does. In the crucible of life, jolted by daily experiences, Christian faith broadens and deepens. We learn that meditation, a deepening prayer life, and reflective study on God's Word will take us into areas that are almost unimaginable. In our relationship with God, we can get miles beyond memorizing the Ten Commandments and singing "Kumbaya." How? *Prokopto.*

Last is what Luke tags as "favor with man." Call it social growth or learning how to get along with people. It includes everything from developing good manners to learning how to build rapport with friends and family. Social skills are the lubricant of life, the stuff from which civilized conduct grows. It keeps us all from becoming grouchy old men and mean old women.

None of those four growth areas are easy to master, if mastered at all. We keep working in each area our whole life. *Prokopto.* So what should we do about all this?

First, put *prokopto* into your life plan. Each of these areas in which Jesus *prokopto*-ed calls to us. Get into—and stay with—the intellectual/physical/spiritual/social dynamic. Explore everything. Start with listing what you are doing to improve your mind. Have you read any books lately? Have you considered participating in an elderhostel as a way to study something "just because"? Have you done a crossword puzzle? Have you traveled with an educational purpose?

How about your body? You can limber joints and muscles each day, but there's more. Who says you can't learn to swim at 70, walk two miles, or learn new eating habits? Do it. *Prokopto*!

Ever thought of maintaining a spiritual journal filled with your observations on the goodness of God and the wonder of grace? Have you been on a spiritual retreat? What about asking your pastor for ways to get more out of Sunday morning? You might stir him to put more in. He's under the *prokopto* umbrella too.

Are your social skills beyond improvement? Then try listening to your spouse for a day while keeping the ear/mouth ratio (*two* ears, *one* mouth) in mind. People in polite society do things like that.

You know what happens? $4 \times 1 = 5$. A fifth gift attaches to the intellectual/physical/spiritual/social quartet: emotional health. People who *prokopto* the first four get the fifth as a bonus.

Prayer Suggestion: Ask God for the will and energy to *prokopto*.

For Reflection

- Now that you've heard the advice, what will you do to *prokopto*? Write down ideas and share them with someone who might join you.
- Is there something new you've wanted to do for a long time? Is it possible for you to do it now? What might you substitute if it's impossible for you to accomplish this item?

Charles S. Mueller Sr.

Power to Believe

I am not ashamed of the gospel, because it is the power of God for the salvation of everyone who believes.

Romans 1:16

How did Jesus turn water to wine? At the age of 9, I began to understand. How? The same way my brother would rise from the dead. It was a miracle.

Where is this power of God? I did not know much about electricity at the age of 9. We had gas and kerosene lanterns in the parsonage. But I heard of dynamiting rocks to lay a country culvert. I knew how fast our Chevy could go. I knew Mr. Sodman's white mules could pull whatever had to be pulled. How could my brother rise from the dead? That was something only God could do. How it happened was a secret. I believed. That hasn't changed in 60 years. Believing brings rest, peace, safety.

My brother was whistling "A Mighty Fortress Is Our God" as he left the country parsonage. By radio we had just heard Dr. Walter A. Maier preaching on "The

Lutheran Hour," and I was happy to hear again that I was saved. The whistling was Paul's last song on earth. The words of the sermon were in his young mind. He fell from a willow tree in winter into a Nebraska creek. I was 9, and I believed in the miracle at Cana. Now I had a larger miracle to believe—resurrection.

I believed but needed help with my unbelief. The congregation was in our house when our family came home with Paul's shoes and clothes. We saw that he was dead, and now it was supper time. The sun had set, and our family of six had a house full of congregation members. I heard the tears, the silence, new words of farmers, loving words, care, hope. In the kitchen, we ate warm milk poured over toast with salt and pepper. Perhaps we ate more; I don't remember. Father spoke the prayer in German, "The Lord has given. The Lord has taken away. Blessed be the name of the Lord." I did not understand or like the prayer. I was 9 and it seemed the prayer could be said later, not so soon. The word *blessed* seemed too complimentary. My father believed the prayer.

Paul was buried between many graves I knew by heart. There were Bible verses all around him, carved in stone, marble, cement, bronze. Paul had a piece of paper at the head of his grave—his birth and death date typed on it. The earth was fresh, but resurrection could come anytime.

On Saturdays 40 of us children met with father to study God's Word in the white church schoolhouse at the edge of the cemetery. I asked father for a seat by a window where I could watch the grave. If Resurrection Day came soon, I wanted a front-row seat to see Paul rise. All the graves in the cemetery were positioned so the dead would rise facing east. East was toward Mr. Norbrook's farm. East was really all the way to the holy city of Jerusalem. I pictured Jerusalem the Golden, even more beautiful than the Nebraska state capitol. If I leaned left at the window seat, the Bible verse on Pastor Geyer's red marble stone appeared to be on Paul's grave. I borrowed the verse whenever I wished. It was powerful to me. The verse made resurrection more real, especially since Rev. Geyer had been pastor for 40 years before my father. He'd believed the Bible verse, and all 13 Geyer children in the congregation believed in the resurrection from the dead.

Spring came and my brother had not been raised. We planted rose moss on the grave, and his college class gave him a sundial. From that year on, space and time changed for me. Jerusalem the Golden was now closer and bigger than Virgil Norbrook's farm. Easter, Good Friday, and Christmas all came in the same week that Paul died. Winter turning to spring became a miracle. Fear turning to trust was a bigger miracle. Words became worlds, and I got inside them to feel safe. What people did to one another became a word of God. Everything changed, and I could feel the power of God present over the country cemetery.

I drew pictures of Joe Louis, and I hummed "A Mighty Fortress." Joe was the champion boxer of the world, and the hymn was Paul's last song. It was the strongest and loudest song I knew, and what I needed was the "power of God for salvation."

God still turns water to wine, seed to harvest, winter to summer, death to life. I believe the way I did when I was 9, and I still sit at a little country window watching for God's miracles.

Prayer: O God, You are a transforming God whose power is great, always in motion, making everything new. In Your faithfulness, we have the power to believe. In Jesus' name we believe. Amen.

For Reflection

- Look carefully at something specific. See in it how God transformed life. See a tree in motion, turning, changing. See a person in motion, turning, transforming. Watch a feeling in motion, turning, renewing.

- What will you enjoy most about the resurrection?

Herbert Brokering

Consistent Christians

If we were to list those traits we desire in a person, one would most surely be *consistency*. The dictionary defines *consistency* as "keeping to the same principles or course of action." Baseball players like umpires who are consistent in the way they call balls and strikes. Lawyers like judges who are consistent in applying legal principles. We like people who act in consistent ways because they are predictable.

Few people are totally consistent. Everyone strays at times from the principles in which they believe. The great people of our time often are inconsistent. Heroes in the Bible even showed inconsistencies. One of the great prophets of the Old Testament, Samuel, occasionally was inconsistent. In one important way, however, he was totally consistent—he always sought to serve his Lord.

Consecrated to the Lord by his parents when he was young and reared by an aging priest, Samuel devoted his life to serving God. He may not always have acted wisely—as when he appointed his sons to serve as judges—yet the people held him in high regard despite his poor judgment and his sons' evil ways. At God's command, Samuel anointed Saul as the first king of Israel. Later, he boldly confronted King Saul about his disobedience. Samuel was consistent in his service to his Lord. When he died, the Scriptures report that "All Israel assembled and mourned for him" (1 Samuel 25:1). Samuel was a man of God, dedicating his whole life to God's service.

Our Lord is a model of consistency. Most important, He is consistent in His love. From the moment of our birth until now, God has consistently kept us in His loving care. At Baptism, He covenanted with us, promising that He would

- always be our God;
- have a place for us in His heart and heavenly home; and
- make us a blessing to others.

In His great love, God sent Jesus to restore the harmony He intended when He placed Adam and Eve in Eden. He promises life forever to those who remain faithful to Him. All this despite our inconsistencies!

Each of us can look back over the years and recognize God's guiding and protecting hand. Each of us can recall occasions when He used us in His service. Now that we have set aside time to enjoy our "chronological giftedness," we have additional opportunities to emulate Samuel in serving God. Who knows how many people we have touched, or how many more we may touch, with the Good News of Jesus Christ?

As Samuel was consistent in service to his Lord, may we also be consistent as we live in the days to come.

Prayer Suggestion: Take a moment to reflect on God's consistent love and care in your life. Thank Him for His many blessings. Ask Him to show you new opportunities in which you may touch other people with Jesus Christ for healing and service.

For Reflection

- Think about times when you are most likely to be inconsistent. What does this tell you about yourself? What help do you need to overcome this inconsistency?

- Is there a senior adult organization in your church or community that can use your talents or skills to enhance the quality of life for other individuals? Check with your pastor or other civic leaders for a niche you can fill.

Fred A. Meyer

None of the Above?

Have you heard the story of a young college graduate applying for a position with the United States government? Filling out the application form, he came across the question, "Do you favor the overthrow of the U.S. government by force, violence, rebellion, or other unlawful means?" Conditioned by hundreds of multiple-choice tests, he blithely answered, "Other unlawful means."

When we review our lives as Christians, sometimes we are tempted to answer spiritual questions in a similar manner. For example:

In evaluating the "sufficiency" of my faith life, do I

- love my neighbor as myself?
- cheerfully and generously support my local fellowship of believers?
- share my joy in the Lord with those who do not know Him?
- pray for the person who has wronged me?
- keep in touch with the Lord's will by daily searching His Word?

Human nature tempts us to put priorities on our faith life, listing those first that seem easier. Or we may ignore the difficult responses to God's love altogether. But priorities such as these are not God's priorities. His holiness already has been satisfied without adding our works to it—even works of praise. What is it that we must do? God's answer? "None of the above." Strange, isn't it?

This is a difficult lesson for believers. We can add nothing to what our Lord already has declared complete. Does this mean that we can forget about doing good works? About serving our neighbors? About loving the unlovable? About testifying to our faith? About simply "doing the right thing"?

No. And yes.

We need not fret about "doing enough." God assures us that salvation and reconciliation are complete—that Jesus did it all. The answer, in its most important sense, is "No, we do not have to be concerned." But there is a yes to the question that can be illustrated by another anecdote.

A kindergarten teacher took her class into the church so she could explain the symbols. The group first passed the baptismal font where, in a very winning way, the teacher explained that here people are first brought to Jesus and made part of God's family. All their sins are washed away.

The little group continued the tour, looking at the stained-glass windows and learning the stories they illustrated or symbolized. The teacher explained the altar and the liturgical colors of the paraments. On the way out, passing the baptismal font again, one of her streetwise children asked, "Does that thing really work?"

That is the real question—the best question because it has the best answer.

We rehearse our Baptism each day (don't we?) so the temptation to sin and our past sins can be "drowned." In this "newness of life," we live renewed lives. And those lives are the lives of thankful works, of joyful works, of enthusiastic service as our response to a living God who has done it all already.

Mysterious? Yes.

Wonderful? Of course!

A good friend once said, "It's so easy being a Christian." Her thought is quite correct, but it is incomplete. Beginning the day with a renewal of our baptismal vow gives us great impetus for service. There's work to be done in God's creation and among His creatures.

Does Baptism really work? Yes, in of itself, and then in the lives and works of the redeemed.

Prayer Suggestion: Pray for discernment in your view of works as they relate to faith. Also pray for a responsive heart to those in need, whether material or spiritual, and a willingness to serve both them and a loving God.

For Reflection

- St. Paul does an excellent job of revealing the complex relationship between faith and works in the book of Romans. Give yourself a treat. Read and meditate on a chapter each day. Sixteen days from now, you'll be happy you did.

- What do you do to remember your Baptism? What can you do to remember it more often?

Wayne Lucht

How Old Are You?

Lord, You have been our dwelling place in all generations. … For a thousand years in Your sight are like yesterday when it is past, or like a watch in the night. … The days of our life are seventy years, or perhaps eighty, if we are strong; even then their span is only toil and trouble; they are soon gone, and we fly away.

Psalm 90:1, 4, 10 (NRSV)

Do you read the obituary column? Most older people will admit that they read the list daily. I said I'd never do it. But I did this morning and yesterday morning. I probably will read it again tomorrow.

Why do we read the obituary column? We may say it's because we wouldn't want to miss a friend's funeral. The truth is that if a friend died, someone would let us know. I remember checking out the obits on a regular basis after I attended several funerals for people younger than I. If they had died in an accident, that would have seemed logical. But they had died of heart disease and other things that I always had associated with old age.

I'll be honest. When I read the list of those who have died, I pay little attention to names. I look for dates. Was the person born before or after me? I don't pay much attention to those who died very young—in their 30s or younger. I watch for those who were less than 10 years younger than I. Nor do I pay much attention to those who lived to be 98 or 100. That's beyond my present horizon. I do keep score on those who were five, 10, or 15 years older than I when they died. I feel free to admit this because I know lots of other people do the same thing. What is this thing we have about our age?

When young people lie about their age, they add a few years. Middle-aged people usually "miscalculate" by forgetting a few birthdays. Some older people start fudging again by making themselves older than their legal age.

How do you feel about your age? Many times we say, "I don't feel like I am ____." I admit that I don't feel like the age printed on my driver's license. I've figured that I am not the same as my father was when he was my age. He wore his body out through physical work on the farm. He did not have the medical care that has been available to me. You may think the same thing. We don't feel like we think our parents felt at this age.

On my 33rd birthday, I realized that I was as old as

Jesus when He died. From then on, I was older than He had ever been. Part of Jesus' earthly life was to become a human being. That meant He experienced part of the aging system. But age is not a part of His identity. He has been the Son of God since time began. He is part of the future that reaches beyond measured time.

Jesus became a part of the age system so He could live for us the perfect life God expected. First, He had to be listed with the newborns. If the *Bethlehem Daily News* had been in existence, He would have been named as the son of Joseph and Mary. Later, He would have been listed in the obituary column—executed at 33.

Because of His life, Jesus added a new column to those that record the events of life. The new column would be titled "Resurrections." That list has not been published yet. But God is getting it ready. "And I saw the dead, small and great, stand before God; and the books were opened: and another book was opened, which is the book of life" (Revelation 20:12a KJV).

Prayer: Lord Jesus Christ, be with me now and on the day of my death so I may be with You in the day that has no end. Amen.

For Reflection

- Do you read the obituaries? What response might you offer because of Jesus when you read the notice of a Christian burial?

- Does your newspaper announce births? What role can you play in the growth of those children—even without leaving your chair?

Eldon Weisheit

Here Am I Lord— Send Him!

With so many needs and problems in the world, do you ever wish that more people would do something about them? I do. If only more of "those" people would care for others. If only more of "those" people would volunteer time in their congregation and community. Then one day I realized that I am one of "those" people!

Do you realize that every eight seconds from now until the end of the year 2014 someone in the United States will turn 50? By 2050, an estimated 100 million men and women, or 20 percent of our population, will be over 65. The age-wave continues to explode. What power we have as older adults! Yet, in my weaker moments, I still mutter, "Here am I Lord—send him."

Perhaps we need a T-shirt that reads: "Bold—as in old!" God gave us life to serve Him and to share with others. We need to be bold about living for God. Down with activities that help us "get away from it all." Forget about the "been there—done that" philosophy. Instead, share your faith and your life and your experiences with more young people.

Mike Krzyzewski, Duke University's basketball coach, recently told a group of retired persons that they represented experience, wisdom, and expertise. As older people, they had responsibilities to the younger members of society. He asked everyone to think of ways to make their community a better place. He received a standing ovation.

Older adults may not have more responsibility for society, but neither do they have less. Instead of waiting for someone to ask, perhaps we need to volunteer more emphatically: "Here am I, send me!" If it worked for Isaiah, it will work for us! Listen again to God's Word: "Then I heard the voice of the Lord saying, 'Whom shall I send? And who will go for Us?' And I said, 'Here am I. Send me!'" (Isaiah 6:8).

By the power of the Spirit, we can be "bold—as in old!" Talk to a 6-year-old next week at church. Call your pastor to share an affirming word. Compliment whoever delivers your newspaper on ever-improving aim. Smile and wave to the young upstart who just cut you off in traffic. Volunteer to teach vacation Bible school next summer. Offer to visit with a couple that is contemplating marriage. And on and on, as the Lord sends you to a daily ministry of joy and hope.

Here am I, Lord. Do send him, but also send me!

Prayer Suggestion: Ask the Lord to forgive you for times you refused to be "sent." Ask Him for the power of the Holy Spirit as He now sends you to share health and hope with others.

For Reflection

- List five specific things you can do to help someone this week. Go ahead, give it a try. Remember, the Lord is sending you!

- Allow or invite someone to help you. You both need practice!

Rich Bimler

Worried? Try V-A-D

As we look back at our lives—thinking about parents, neighbors and friends, people in our church, former coworkers, and children—one reality we come to accept is that worry is universal. There is no worry-free age. We begin to worry as soon as we're old enough to think of ourselves as individuals, and worry continues throughout life.

Worry, of course, can be harmful, especially because it so often involves things over which we have no control. Worry can sour our disposition, paralyze our spirit, and disrupt our Christian service. Worry causes or intensifies physical disorders. When we're worried, we can't enjoy life.

What can we do about worry? How do mature, senior Christians respond? What advice do we offer to others? Based on the words of Jesus, I'd like to suggest the V-A-D formula.

The basis for V-A-D is found in the Sermon on the Mount. Jesus says:

> *Therefore I tell you, do not worry about your life, what you will eat or drink; or about your*

*body, what you will wear. Is not life more
important than food, and the body more
important than clothes? Look at the birds of
the air; they do not sow or reap or store away
in barns, and yet your heavenly Father feeds
them. Are you not much more valuable than
they? Who of you by worrying can add a single hour of his life? … But seek first His
kingdom and His righteousness, and all
these things will be given to you as well.
Matthew 6:25–27, 33*

V stands for *value*. To paraphrase Jesus: "Worried?
Value yourself." Value yourself in the light of God's love.
Aren't you worth more to God than any other creature?

When we worry, we forget the extent of God's love.
If He cares for birds and flowers, how much more will
He care for us! We're not lovable, but God loved us
enough to send His Son to suffer and die that we might
be saved.

When we worry about ourselves, we can examine
God's love. As we grow older, we may be tempted to feel
we are no longer of much value. But God made us special through Jesus Christ. By His power, we can fight
worry as we value ourselves as His children.

A stands for *accept*. Jesus said: "Who of you by worrying can add a single hour of his life?" Our Lord says
to accept yourself as you are and for what you are—
God's child, an old "geezer" but God's valuable child.
Jesus tells you not to worry about things you can't

change. A widely repeated prayer encourages us to pray, "God, grant me the serenity to accept the things I cannot change, courage to change the things I can, and wisdom to know the difference."

It takes strength and humility to accept our limitations, weaknesses, and strengths rather than to worry about them. When we see our limitations and weaknesses, what are we tempted to do? We may try to hide our weaknesses, then worry that we haven't hidden them well enough. Or we scoff. We say it's really not important. Then we worry because we *do* care. Or we run away. We refuse to let others accept us, and we refuse to let God use our talents.

It's equally difficult to accept our strengths, many of which have resulted from years of experience. It's difficult to accept strengths for what they are—gifts of God—and to use them for Him. The devil tempts us to use these gifts to dominate or to manipulate others or for our own gain or glory. We can never get enough glory or gain to satisfy our sinful self.

When we worry, we can ask, "Am I accepting myself as I am—a child of God? Am I being honest with myself? Am I permitting God to reveal my strengths and my limitations?" When we allow God to take care of us, He blesses us. He helps us accept ourselves as forgiven sinners. He helps us grow, even in our later years. He helps us maintain a positive attitude, and He helps us overcome worry.

D stands for *dedicate*. Jesus says: "But seek first His kingdom and His righteousness, and all these things will be given to you as well" (Matthew 6:33). God is the only one who will not disappoint us. If we dedicate ourselves first to family, goods, church, annuities, security, intellect, pensions, or our own ability, we're doomed to disappointment. We will worry even more.

Seeking God's kingdom means putting Him first in our affection, in our interests, in our schedule. We can't do any of this alone. We need God's help. When we're worried, we can ask, "What am I putting first in my life?" When it's God and His kingdom, we don't need to worry because God promises to give us all we need for life in His kingdom.

To review the formula that relieves worry, we should *V*—value ourselves in relationship to God's love; *A*—accept ourselves for what we are through God's gifts and grace; *D*—dedicate ourselves to God and His kingdom. It's only through God's gift that we rightly value, accept, and dedicate ourselves.

Prayer Suggestion: Talk with God about your worries. Be sure to thank Him for His love and ask His blessings according to His will.

For Reflection

- Who shares worries with you? How do you usually respond? Is there a better response?
- Think back to former worries. How did God help you with them? How would the V-A-D formula have helped?

Les Bayer

God, I Need You!

Read Psalm 46

Hospital stays are filled with anxiety, boredom, loneliness, and often pain. Soon after admittance, you're flat on your back, and you begin to lose your sense of control. When people approach you, they look down with an assuring smile, but you don't know what they are thinking about or what they are going to do to you. You have even signed papers that give them control, absolving them of blame should something go wrong.

Others are now in charge of your body, your schedule—everything. They touch, probe, prick, invade, and sometimes cut and staple. Most of the time, you don't know what to expect next. Helpful caregivers explain, but it still hurts.

Waiting, waiting, always waiting—in your room for the next exam, in the corridor for your next test. People walk by wearing sympathetic smiles as they hurry about their business. You wait for the test results, for the nurse to change your IV, for the aide to help you to the washroom.

Though people are constantly around you, you feel alone. Thoughts about your illness and treatment often turn inward. You might even feel that God has forgotten you. You know you're not supposed to feel that way, but there is that internal voice that wonders just where God is.

It's comforting to know that David had the same thoughts. In Psalm 13, he wrote about feeling abandoned by God. He wavered in his trust. David asked: "How long must I wrestle with my thoughts?" (verse 2) He thought he wasn't getting an answer or, at least, not the right answer. He wanted "light to my eyes," (verse 3)—some decisive action by God or some reason for the wait.

But David's faith and trust broke through the gloom in the final verses, "But I trust in Your unfailing love; my heart rejoices in Your salvation. I will sing to the LORD, for He has been good to me" (verses 5–6). David had experienced the blessings of God in his past. God had made him a child of the covenant. God's Word assured him of His presence, the same presence God had always shown.

David is considered a hero of the faith, but not because he didn't sin. We know he did, and more important, David knew he had sinned. He turned to God in repentance, asking forgiveness. And David was forgiven. We also know that his trust in God occasionally wavered. But God would not let go of David. God renewed his faith and trust.

When we feel vulnerable, as we often do when

we're sick, we can turn to God for comfort and assurance. Because of faith in God and in His Son, we can call on Him who is ever present to help us in all our needs.

No matter what our level of spiritual maturity, God sees and hears our worship and prayers. Times of trauma provide a vigorous spiritual checkup. Were we prepared for the spiritual impact of a hospital experience, or for that matter, any intense confrontation with crisis or pain?

We can review times in our life and identify God's hand in resolving painful issues. His Word gave direction; He effected change in others, in us, in the situation. His wisdom prevailed over our feeble efforts, and He rescued us.

Most hospital stays end with recovery. The waiting and the pain cease. The Savior's healing hand has been on us again. It's back into the world with God at our side.

Prayer: Dear Father in heaven, I look back and testify of Your loving presence in my life. I recall Your control of my past for my good. Keep me close to You, I pray. Help me remain faithful to You and to Your Son. In my Savior's name. Amen.

For Reflection

- Recall God's presence during difficult times in your life.
- Give yourself a spiritual checkup:
    - ❏ study of God's Word
    - ❏ worship attendance
    - ❏ prayer life

Ed Krueger

Retiring from Retirement

I do not claim that I have already succeeded or have already become perfect. I keep striving to win the prize for which Christ Jesus has already won me to Himself. Of course, my brothers, I really do not think that I have already won it; the one thing I do, however, is to forget what is behind me and do my best to reach what is ahead. So I run straight toward the goal in order to win the prize, which is God's call through Christ Jesus to the life above.

Philippians 3:12–14 (TEV)

Did you spend most of your life getting ready for the future? Many of us did, and I think it's a good way to live. Learn how to live with your parents, brothers, and sisters so you can raise your own family some day. Do your schoolwork so you can get a good job. Work hard so you will be ready for retirement. Eat your carrots and broccoli. Don't eat fat. Get off the couch and exercise. Stop smoking. All in the name of your future! If you live right today, you'll have a better tomorrow.

I finally got there. I'm retired. Social Security and retirement checks arrive every month. All that planning paid off. How about you? Are you retired? If so, maybe you've also discovered something that I learned through others long ago. Retirement does not end our need to plan for the future, and I'm not talking about going to heaven now. Jesus already has planned eternity for us. I'm talking about what happens between now and then.

Think about what you planned for retirement. With minor variations, plans often included things such as finances, living arrangements, part-time or volunteer work, travel, golf, fishing, college courses, time with family, yard work, reading, movies, and losing the alarm clock. Most retired people enjoy the new opportunity to manage their own time and do their own thing. In my part of the country, they call it the "Green Valley grin." (Green Valley is a retirement community south of Tucson, Arizona.)

Those who retire soon realize that initial retirement is not the final step before heaven. Sometimes parents are still alive, and the retirement of an 85-year-old is different than that of one who is 65. We who are newly retired like to brag about how busy we are. We don't know how we ever had time to work. But what happens when we have done all the things on our retirement list? Or what happens when we can't finish the list?

There is a stage of life after retirement. I call it retiring from retirement. It is yet another big change in life—and you thought that adolescence and the change-of-life were a pain! Those who think they can live with the Green Valley grin for the rest of their lives and make no plans for this second retirement will find themselves with the same problem as those who didn't plan for the first retirement.

Retiring from retirement has a different set of needs. Money and time do not hold as high a priority. Travel is off the list for most. The circle of friends becomes much smaller. You forget about lower weight and cholesterol. Those who reach this stage of life still face challenges. Their life still has value to themselves and to others.

Some people who are retired from retirement question why God has left them here. One lady was concerned that her family and friends already in heaven would start to think she hadn't made it. Older retired persons sometimes experience severe pain and overwhelming loneliness. But they still have a future. They still look forward—even if it is to death. They are still running the race that Christ already won for them.

Plan ahead for the next stage of life. Avoid remarks such as, "I'll never live in a nursing home," "I won't get stuck in a wheelchair," "I will not live with my children." If the time comes that you need any of those things, you will be grateful that God has provided them. Keep an open mind about the future because through Jesus Christ you always have one.

Prayer

Now I lay me down to sleep.
I pray the Lord my soul to keep.
If I should die before I wake,
I pray the Lord my soul to take.
If I should wake before I die,
I pray the Lord to show me why.
This I ask for Jesus' sake. Amen.

For Reflection

- Make a "to do" list for your retirement years. Consider what you may have omitted, and add it to your list.

- What provisions can you make now for your future?

Eldon Weisheit

Time Threads

The unrelenting rhythms of the daily work-
world foster a weariness of the hustle and
bustle.
The seasons come and go, and we long to
stay their flight.
The weekly stress speeds life's pulse with
unspoken urgency.

Need a stretch, Lord, need a stretch—that is
ours, all ours—to sniff the flowers and
meadows and listen to whispering choruses
Of the mighty pines under which lie little
generational cones awakening
In the shelter of the mother trees ... ah, Your
sweet mysteries.

The hillsides shout with flowering joy, yet
our flagging hearts and faltering steps often
eclipse the moments.

Why, Lord, does the weight of hustle blind
and bend us so?

*Life's seasons beckon with multiple grace
notes for reflection and a passion for life,
Coupled with the yoke of weights that share
a rhetoric of business, mending and tran-
scending moments, and gentle reminders of
things left to do.
Can it be, Lord,
That our souls struggle to awaken us to Your
enveloping daily mantle
Not only during the transitional ebbtides of
life, but also during the everyday run of the
race?*

*Heaven-sent serendipities thread the tapes-
tries of time.
Hearts sing with fleeting songs of praise that
bestow a joyful peace and an "Amen Silence."*

*Your daily Word provides so many
"wond'rous ah-hahs"
The privilege of worship and respite on Your
seventh day bountifully
Endow the spirit.*

*Your shepherd's presence at all ages and
stages shatters the weights,
Lightens the pace for the allotted gift of days.*

Prayer: Lord Jesus, thank You for Your presence in all the stages of my life. It will be so good to meet You face to face! Amen.

For Reflection

- List the "wond'rous ah-hahs" you've learned from God's Word. Do this by paging through the book of Psalms. Look for poetry that describes your awe and praise.

- If you could share one incident from your life in which God "shattered the weights," what would it be? What weights does He shatter for you now?

Shirley Bergman

Good News

"I bring you good news." Luke 2:10

Read Isaiah 40:9–11 and Luke 24:45–59.

Sometimes "good news" seems to be a contradiction in terms! If you're accustomed to prime time news with its inevitable catalog of murders, rapes, and drive-by shootings, you may not be disposed to call news *good*. But "There is good news tonight," as one commentator from the past used to introduce his nightly report.

There truly is good news, but you might have to visit a cemetery to find it. Often the best news comes from a graveyard. A daffodil blooming alongside a headstone is lovely news—a sign of life after a long, cold winter. The Bible says, "Unless a kernel of wheat falls to the ground and dies, it remains only a single seed. But if it dies, it produces many seeds" (John 12:24).

Christians know that the very best news is news from a cold, stone cave outside the city limits of Jerusalem. The empty tomb of Christ assures us that our sins are forgiven. Death has no sting. The devil has been forever vanquished. You are not as others who have no hope. Christ lives and is with you to the end of the age. Your faith has laid its grip on truth and victory and everlasting life.

Good news about our future comes from the grave of Jesus. The angel at the tomb proclaimed it: "He is not here." Of course He isn't. He's loose in the world. Jesus lives and reigns. Our world is not a huge orphanage filled with Fatherless children. It is not just a whirling ball, hurtling through space, and we its accidental inhabitants. It is the home provided by our Father through His Son—the home in which we are loved and protected by the risen Son of God Himself.

Life is not an accident, but a planned and governed procedure by which Christ Jesus makes us heirs of life eternal. From Jesus' grave comes the news that nothing permanently damaging can happen to us. God will not create another you or find somebody to take your place. In a world where it's easy to become a number, God calls you by your name. The grave of Jesus tells you how far God went to remember your name.

This good news has been around for a long time, but it remains as fresh as this morning's newspaper headlines. Stop for a moment before the empty tomb if you want to hear some good news.

Prayer Suggestion: Pray for those most closely affected by the events recorded in today's headlines.

For Reflection

- Identify several events or issues appearing in your newspaper today that you would classify as bad news. In each case, how could the Good News of Jesus speak comfort or hope?
- Recall your family history. How has God been part of that history?

Arnold Kuntz

Say It Now!

We have been blessed with many exciting people. Remember these words from St. Paul? "I always thank God for you because of His grace given you in Christ Jesus. For in Him you have been enriched in every way"

1 Corinthians 1:4–5

I often take people for granted. The loved ones around me—spouse, kids, grandkids, staff people—seem always to "be there" when I need them. Something struck me as I read the late Mike Royko's columns. After his wife died of a brain aneurysm, he ended one of his articles by urging his readers to tell someone they love the way they feel—and say it right now!

Say it now! Say some encouraging, affirming, and helpful words to all God's people. Who in your life needs a word of comfort, hope, or love? Don't put it off—say it now! Who might be overjoyed to receive a phone call from you? Call now! Who might be waiting at the mailbox for some good news? Write today.

Through the years, pastors have spoken eloquent

words at funerals. We hear that Uncle George did wonderful things during his life. These words are comforting and helpful to George's friends and family, but George probably would have enjoyed hearing them firsthand!

Throughout the New Testament, St. Paul encourages us with strong words of affirmation and love. He was truly an encourager—bringing words of affirmation and hope to people just like you and me who struggled in their lives. Throughout the pain and struggle, St. Paul reminds us that there is hope—in Jesus Christ. Paul "says it now," not just to share words, but to share faith in the Lord. Christ's death and resurrection give us the hope and the power to share our new life with those around us—beginning today!

There's no need to wallow in the past when we failed to speak words of comfort and hope. Start today, and continue each day, to say words of love and hope and joy and peace to those around you.

So what do we say to people? Why not start with phrases such as, "I love you," "I appreciate you," "You are special to me." Then let your mind and imagination take over! We also can share words of hope by reminding people of God's love for all of us. We can share powerful words from Scripture, such as "May the God of hope fill you with all joy and peace as you trust in Him, so that you may overflow with hope by the power of the Holy Spirit" (Romans 15:13).

We continue to thank the Lord for those around us who love and care for us. We can continue to share our faith and hope because our Lord Jesus Christ gives us power and occasion to "say it now."

Prayer Suggestion: Thank the Lord for the special people around you. Thank God for the love and care and joy they share with you. Thank God for His presence, which enables you to love others in His name!

For Reflection

- Who has shown special care for you? What have they said or done to make you feel special? What can you learn from them as you interact with others?

- During the next five days, intentionally offer specific words of comfort and hope to two of your special people each day. Tell them you love them. Tell them the Lord loves them. Say it now!

Rich Bimler

Praise the Lord!

Read the following aloud.

But you are a chosen people, a royal priest-hood, a holy nation, a people belonging to God, that you may declare the praises of Him who called you out of darkness into His wonderful light. Once you were not a people, but now you are the people of God; once you had not received mercy, but now you have received mercy.

1 Peter 2:9–10

I will sing to the LORD all my life; I will sing praise to my God as long as I live. May my meditation be pleasing to Him, as I rejoice in the LORD.

Psalm 104:33–34

Sing joyfully to the LORD, you righteous; it is fitting for the upright to praise Him. Praise the LORD with the harp; make music to Him

*on the ten-stringed lyre. Sing to Him a new
song; play skillfully, and shout for joy. For the
word of the LORD is right and true; He is faithful in all He does. The LORD loves righteousness and justice; the earth is full of His
unfailing love. Sing joyfully to the LORD,
you righteous; it is fitting for the upright to
praise Him.*

Psalm 33:1–5; 1

*I love the LORD, for He heard my voice; He
heard my cry for mercy. Because He turned
His ear to me, I will call on Him as long as I
live. The cords of death entangled me, the
anguish of the grave came upon me; I was
overcome by trouble and sorrow. Then I
called on the name of the LORD, "O LORD,
save me!" The LORD is gracious and righteous; our God is full of compassion. The
LORD protects the simplehearted; when I was
in great need, He saved me. ... How can I
repay the LORD for all His goodness to me?
... I will sacrifice a thank offering to You and
call on the name of the LORD. I will fulfill my
vows to the LORD in the presence of all His
people, in the courts of the house of the
LORD—in your midst, O Jerusalem. Praise
the LORD.*

Psalm 116:1–6, 12, 17–19

I will praise you, O LORD, with all my heart; I will tell of all Your wonders. I will be glad and rejoice in You; I will sing praises to Your name, O Most High. ... The LORD reigns forever; He has established His throne for judgment. He will judge the world in righteousness; He will govern the peoples with justice. The LORD is a refuge for the oppressed, a stronghold in times of trouble. Those who know Your name will trust in You, for You, LORD, have never forsaken those who seek You. Sing praises to the LORD, enthroned in Zion; proclaim among the nations what He has done.

Psalm 9:1–2, 7–11

It is good to praise the LORD and make music to Your name, O Most High, to proclaim Your love in the morning and Your faithfulness at night, to the music of the ten-stringed lyre and the melody of the harp. For You make me glad by Your deeds, O LORD; I sing for joy at the works of Your hands. How great are Your works, O LORD, how profound Your thoughts! ... It is good to praise the LORD and make music to Your name, O Most High.

Psalm 92:1–5; 1

Praise be to You, O LORD, God of our father Israel, from everlasting to everlasting. Yours, O LORD, is the greatness and the power and the glory and the majesty and the splendor, for everything in heaven and earth is Yours. Yours, O LORD, is the kingdom; You are exalted as head over all. Wealth and honor come from You; You are the ruler of all things. In Your hands are strength and power to exalt and give strength to all. Now, our God, we give You thanks, and praise Your glorious name.

1 Chronicles 29:10b–13

May God be gracious to us and bless us and make His face shine upon us, that Your ways may be known on earth, Your salvation among all nations. May the peoples praise You, O God; may all the peoples praise You. May the nations be glad and sing for joy, for You rule the peoples justly and guide the nations of the earth. May the peoples praise You, O God; may all the peoples praise You. Then the land will yield its harvest, and God, our God, will bless us. God will bless us, and all the ends of the earth will fear Him.

Psalm 67

Glory be to the Father and to the Son
And to the Holy Spirit;
As it was in the beginning, is now,
And will be forever. Amen.

Prayer: Thank You, Lord, for recording the words of praise I read today. Thank You for a voice to speak them aloud, as they were spoken centuries ago. Now give me words of my own that I, too, may praise You from my heart. Amen.

For Reflection

- For what blessings can you praise God? Say a two- or three-sentence prayer of praise.
- Share your words of praise with someone special.

Ed Krueger

Spreading Peanut Butter

This story is about two men—we'll call them Tom and Joe—who worked in a factory and often ate lunch together. Tom hated peanut butter. One noon, Tom took out his first sandwich. It was peanut butter. He stuffed it back inside the box and took out the second sandwich. It was ham and cheese. He smiled and ate. Then Tom took out the last sandwich. He opened it cautiously. It was peanut butter. Tom slammed it back into the box, complaining loudly.

Joe smiled and said, "Tom, you told me that you've been married for 15 years now. Doesn't your wife know that you don't like peanut butter?"

Tom got an angry look on his face and said, "You leave my wife out of this! I made those sandwiches myself."

This story makes life more tolerable when I begin complaining about something. When I honestly examine the situation, quite often I realize that I and my generation have spread much of the "peanut butter" ourselves.

Recently I was with a person I had taught in school many years ago. He was unhappy about the music in his congregation, and he was angry at the pastor. As he talked, I realized that I had spread the "peanut butter" by the narrow views I had once advocated about church music. I had taught him to think the way he did!

Many complaints about young people, prejudices, politics, and the environment are probably a partial result of our peanut butter spreading. I know that often I am too ready to blame others or outside events for my problems. Too often I fail to see the irony in complaining about something that I helped to create.

In Romans 14:12 we read, "So then, each of us will give an account of himself to God." Did you catch the words "of himself"? God loves us as individuals. Christ died for us as individuals. He calls us as individuals to live with Him in eternity. And as He does all this, He gives us the opportunity to be individuals in our service to Him—to assume individual responsibility, with His blessings, and as His children to give an individual account.

We can remind ourselves of this beautiful relationship with God when we are tempted to assign blame for our problems. We tend to forget our own individual responsibility and act as if we are not involved. We forget the joy of individual responsibility.

I once visited a college class where an instructor had just returned some papers. I wanted to speak with the instructor after the class and waited while several students talked with him. Two young women in the class had been sitting directly in front of me. When the class ended, one of them said excitedly to the other, "I got an *A*." The other young woman didn't respond. Finally, the first asked, "What did you get?" After a pause, the woman answered, "He gave me a *C*." That seemed to say it all. **I** got an *A*. **He** gave me a *C*.

As we make daily decisions, we can answer the question, "What peanut butter might I be spreading by this action?" The answer will bring decisions into perspective. When we become upset and complain and blame others, we also can ask, "How much is my fault, and what should I do about it?" With God's guidance, we can bring our individual responsibility into clearer focus, find the real joy of responsibility, and avoid similar pitfalls in the future.

How might we help others benefit by our "peanut butter" experiences? There are three, and only three, superior ways to teach this: (1.) By example. (2.) By example. (3.) By example. As we take responsibility for our actions and for past peanut butter situations, as we clearly show the joy of individual responsibility, as we turn to our Lord for guidance, we become examples to those around us.

God continues to provide opportunities to "make more sandwiches." He provides the bread and ham. He'll help us become more responsible, loving, and joyful children as we trust in Him. He will offer His loving forgiveness for the peanut butter incidents of the past.

Prayer Suggestion: Think of people through whose example God has brought special blessings. Give thanks for these people.

For Reflection

- Send a note to someone expressing your gratitude that he or she has been an example for you. If the person has died, send a note telling of your experience to any relative you can locate.
- What "peanut butter" incident do you most regret? If you're still feeling guilty, lay it before Jesus, who freely forgives.

Les Bayer

You're Special

But you are a chosen people, a royal priest-hood, a holy nation, a people belonging to God, that you may declare the praises of Him who called you out of darkness into His wonderful light. Once you were not a people, but now you are the people of God; once you had not received mercy, but now you have received mercy.

1 Peter 2:9–10

A number of years ago an offer appeared in a San Diego newspaper. It said that anyone who could explain why he or she was average in under 25 words would be listed in new book called *Who's Nobody in America*. The publisher of this book would also put out another entitled *I'm Average, You're Average, and We're Both Okay.*

Perhaps the advertisement was tongue-in-cheek, but it's a sadly accurate and tragic description of many people in our world. After all, we live in a world of nearly six billion people and in a nation of more than one quarter billion. Sometimes it seems as though we goof up more often than we perform heroic deeds. Even at our best, how can we leave even a small mark on history? More important, how or why will the great God of the universe notice us, much less care? Maybe we should get our names on the register of *Who's Nobody in America.*

That's a depressing view of life—and inaccurate! Cheer up. Our life in Christ make us somebodies. St. Peter writes: "Once you were not a people, but now you are the people of God" (1 Peter 2:10). That means we are people precious to God. We're not just little checks in God's big ledger or little punches on a computer card. Instead, God says, "I have summoned you by name; you are Mine" (Isaiah 43:1). St. Peter repeated the thoughts of Isaiah when he wrote, "You are a chosen people, a royal priesthood, a holy nation, a people belonging to God" (1 Peter 2:9).

I've always been fascinated by the way Jesus gathered His disciples. These men didn't thumb through want ads in the *Jerusalem Gazette* and, after weighing various options, decide to apply as a "Disciple of Christ." It was the other way around. Jesus reminded His disciples, "You did not choose Me, but I chose you … to go and bear fruit" (John 15:16). He came to unlikely people in unlikely places and simply said, "Follow Me." Why? Because He had great things for them to do.

God has called you and me in the same way and for the same purpose. We might not consider ourselves heroes of faith. Who among us would claim to be like Peter, James, or John? But don't miss the similarities. None of us chose Jesus. As Martin Luther wrote in his explanation to the Third Article of the Apostles' Creed, it was the Holy Spirit who "called [us] by the Gospel, enlightened [us] with His gifts, sanctified and kept [us] in the true faith." And by the power of the Spirit, we can respond, "Just as I am, without one plea But that thy blood was shed for me And that thou bidd'st me come to thee, O Lamb of God, I come, I come."

Just as I am! That's not a put-down. It's the identifying confession of God's chosen people. "Just as I am" means that I come to Him because He chose me despite my weaknesses and sinfulness. No pretenses, no ungodly boasting or false humility. I am what I am because of God's grace and mercy! By faith, what I am is an individual precious to my God and chosen for His purpose. I am as righteous as any saint could possibly be. Just as I am—empowered to "declare the praises of Him who called You out of darkness into His wonderful light" (1 Peter 2:9).

What God has done for us through Christ Jesus enables us to walk as children of the Light. But how do we walk in the Light and proclaim His praise? To "declare His praises" means to let the glory, majesty, love, and compassion of God show in all we do and say. We might suspect in our own heart, "That's easy for some to say. If I could speak like angels or preach like Paul, I could say it too. If I could go with the missionaries to far-away places, I could really show forth the praises of God. If I could give millions of dollars to build churches or train pastors and teachers, if I could lead large evangelistic campaigns, then I could really be somebody. If I had the energy and stamina and bright-eyed vision of my youth, then I could really make a difference."

God assures us that those are not the criteria for "showing forth His praises." The light that shines through us does not depend on our position or circumstance. It shines forth *from* us because of the Light that shines *in* us. It might shine in simple words or acts of kindness or in humble witness as we visit with a neighbor. It might shine in fervent intercessory prayer for someone in need of a special measure of God's grace. We simply take what the Lord has given and share it with others. Praise God!

Prayer Suggestion: Review your life during the past week. Thank God for opportunities you had to praise Him. Ask for strength to let your light—and His glory—shine more brightly every day.

For Reflection

- Choose one or two people with whom God has placed you in contact—people who need to know the love of God—and call them, send them a note, or arrange for a visit, just to let them know that you care.

- What blessings has God given you to share with others? Identify someone in need with whom you can match your blessings.

August Mennicke

153

"No Fishing Allowed"

Remember not the sins of my youth and my rebellious ways; according to Your love remember me, for You are good, O LORD.

Psalm 25:7

Can you relate to the following event? The new day starts at midnight, but instead of beginning the day with restful sleep, the mind keeps working and you are wide awake. Events of the past flash through your mind. There is the vivid scene of a nasty family argument several years ago. Words were spoken that should not have been said. Emotions ran wild, and vicious words still ring in your ears. It was a dreadful experience. Later, the broken relationships were healed, but you still remember the event. Someone said, "Sticks and stones can break my bones, but names can never hurt me." That doesn't seem to be true because you just can't forget, especially during the night.

The psalmists frequently indicate that such pain is not uncommon. They use phrases such as "Out of the depths I cry to You, O LORD" (Psalm 130:1). Or as Isaiah writes, "For our offenses are many in Your sight, and our sins testify against us" (Isaiah 59:12).

As we reflect on the past, we regretfully recall decisions that negatively affected ourselves and other people. But "If we confess our sins, He is faithful and just and will forgive us our sins and purify us from all unrighteousness" (1 John 1:9). By the grace of God, and through the power of the Holy Spirit, we know and believe that Jesus is our personal Savior. All our sins are forgiven, so we are at peace with God. We also can be at peace with ourselves and others. How blessed we are because of God's love for us!

The devil loves to sow seeds of doubt in our minds. He asks, "Does God really forgive that sin of the past too?" There are times when we immediately say yes, and we remember that God says, "The blood of Jesus, His Son, purifies us from all sin" (1 John 1:7). What a relief it is to have this powerful weapon against such attacks!

What can we do to forget sins that God already has forgotten? Reflect on God's Word of comfort, reread the verse from Psalm 25, or listen to someone assure you of forgiveness. To make this practical, a person once used this example: God took our sins and, through Christ Jesus, paid the price for them. He then buried them in the deepest part of a lake and posted a large sign with the words: "No Fishing." An interesting thought! Don't try to catch the old sins. Don't even remember them. God says that He "remembers your sins no more" (Isaiah 43:25). With these thoughts, we can confidently live this new day. "If the Son sets you free, you will be free indeed" (John 8:36). God's inner peace is in us, and with freedom from eternal consequences of sin, we can reflect His love in our activities today.

Prayer Suggestion: Thank God for His complete forgiveness. Ask Him for more opportunities to reflect His love.

For Reflection

- How would you assure someone of the forgiveness of sins?
- What motivates us to lead lives that are pleasing to our Lord?
- Does maturing in years automatically mean we sin less?

Roy Brockopp

Re-tire or Re-tread?

How does one retire? From work, that is.

For anyone who has tried it, the answer is not as simple as it may seem at first. After the initial weeks of sleeping a little later than usual, taking a more leisurely pace reading the morning newspaper, puttering in the garden, chatting with available neighbors, then ... what?

Even for those whose hobbies offer endless possibilities "if only we had the time," the sameness of the diet can wear thin. Golfing, fishing, travel—all good activities—can consume only part of our available time.

Now what?

Well-intentioned advice to "get involved" or "get outside of yourself" does not easily move us to surrender this precious time of life. Nor does it quiet the unease that creeps into our spirit when some volunteer activities would bring us into contact with people from backgrounds different than our own.

We're reminded of the kindergarten teacher who told her little group about the Good Samaritan in the hopes that they would see the satisfaction of helping others. Her description of the man who fell among thieves who stripped him, beat him, and left him a bloody mess served as a graphic prelude to her question: "What would you have done if you had passed by that poor person?"

Almost without pause, 5-year-old Kathy blurted out, "I'd have thrown up!"

Her honesty startles us, doesn't it? Might we not feel sickened after volunteering at a homeless shelter or tutoring a disadvantaged child from an impoverished neighborhood? If the truth be told, wouldn't we feel a little like Kathy?

Have you realized the difficulty of implementing this piece of wisdom: "The more you give, the more you get"? Our Lord gives us more than a hint of this insight in Malachi 3:10, where He promises to pour out blessings beyond our ability to count them, if we don't choke off our own free giving. In our retirement years, giving of that precious commodity, time, falls under this same promise.

Giving of ourselves brings to us the greatest blessings of all. The reason for this can be explained in two ways. One, it is God-pleasing and God-ordained that giving of ourselves is a priceless blessing of living under the Gospel. Second, life takes on a meaning that simply is not there otherwise. This truth was well expressed by the philosopher who said, "He who has a why to live can bear with almost any how."

Wisdom is not the exclusive property of any generation. Children often offer great insights. Eight-year-old Peter was explaining the church service to younger brother David. But David knew far more than Peter anticipated—the golden plates received money; the man in the pulpit was the pastor; we sing hymns. But Peter had a trump card. He challenged David by asking, "At the end of the service, the pastor says some words and makes a sign. Do you know what that sign means?"

David was stumped.

Peter triumphantly explained, "Some of you people go out that door, some of you go out that door, and some of you go out that door." Truly, we go out under the sign of the cross in everything we do, even as we serve others.

Prayer Suggestion: Discuss your potential service to others with the Lord, who gave Himself totally to others—including you, especially you.

For Reflection

- Examine your community or congregation for activities that depend on volunteers. Don't get immediately involved, but think of what abilities or gifts or personality traits you have and the time in your schedule that you could give. After prayerful thought, consider how God wants you to serve.

- What specific blessings can you anticipate for yourself if you initiate some new activities?

Wayne Lucht

Transformed by God

Bad habits—all of us have them. The longer we live, the more deeply they become entrenched. They may have become so ingrained that we no longer recognize them for what they are, or we may find it almost impossible to free ourselves from them.

Saul—later called Paul—had some horrible habits that kept him from doing what God wanted. Paul later spoke candidly about his misguided zeal during the years that he had persecuted Christians. Read Acts 22:1–20. Paul confessed:

> *I persecuted the followers of this Way to their death, arresting both men and women and throwing them into prison. ... I went from one synagogue to another to imprison and beat those who believe in You. And when the blood of Your martyr Stephen was shed, I stood there giving my approval and guarding the clothes of those who were killing him.*

> Acts 22:4, 19–20

Paul practiced the worst of bad habits. In one glorious moment, however, God transformed this Christian-hunter into an ardent follower and courageous missionary who traveled the world, seeking to save the lost.

If we honestly evaluate ourselves, we must admit that we not only stray from God's will, we also distract others from God's grace. We need transformation from bad habits to godly habits.

Bad habits are hurtful. Some bad habits directly hurt us and affect others indirectly. Some of these might include overindulging in food or drink, worrying, playing the martyr, feeling self-righteous, being envious or greedy, procrastinating, being driven by selfish ambition, holding grudges, and being compulsively neat or untidy. One might argue that these habits are no one's concern but our own and therefore are of no consequence. When we face reality, we know that they can and do hurt us emotionally, spiritually, and sometimes physically. Consequently, they also affect those who care about us.

Through a different set of bad habits, we hurt others directly and ourselves indirectly. Included here might be gossiping, complaining, always needing to be right, uncontrolled anger, bossiness, impatience, putting others down, and blaming others for our mistakes. These can damage the confidence or reputation of others and will destroy relationships with family members and friends. While none of these habits seem as bad as persecuting Christians, they most certainly deter us from accomplishing God's will.

God—who knows all that we think, say, and do—is displeased with these sins. In God's sight, bad habits are not mere annoyances, but an indication that we remain influenced by sin. With Paul, we confess in anguish, "For I have the desire to do what is good, but I cannot carry it out. For what I do is not the good I want to do; no, the evil I do not want to do—this I keep on doing" (Romans 7:18–19).

This all sounds quite discouraging, doesn't it? So how do we become free from the chains of bad habits, or is it impossible? St. Paul gives us the answer once again. To be transformed, we recognize that our bad habits are part of our sinful nature, by which we are "a prisoner of the law of sin" (Romans 7:23). Next, we lay these bad habits at the feet of Jesus, seeking His forgiveness for the damage they have done. Receiving Christ's forgiveness frees us from bondage to bad habits because "there is now no condemnation for those who are in Christ Jesus, because through Christ Jesus the law of the Spirit of life set me free from the law of sin and death" (Romans 8:1–2).

The Holy Spirit enables us to set aside bad habits because "the Lord is the Spirit, and where the Spirit of the Lord is, there is freedom. And we, who with unveiled faces all reflect the Lord's glory, are being transformed into His likeness with ever-increasing glory, which comes from the Lord, who is the Spirit" (2 Corinthians 3:17–18). The same Spirit who transformed Saul transformed us for a life of commitment and service to Jesus. Bad habits, acknowledged and forgiven, can be overcome, and we can accomplish more for Him and through Him than we could ever hope or imagine.

Prayer Suggestion: Focus on your most troublesome bad habit. Ask forgiveness for the negative effects it has on you and others. Then seek the power of the Holy Spirit in God's Word.

For Reflection

- What is the difference between bad habits and unrepented sin?
- Why is it easy to identify (and condemn) bad habits in others? How can you apply what you learn about the bad habits of others to your situation?

Dorothy Schultz

It Was Only a Serving Dish

[Jesus said,] "Do not store up riches for yourselves here on earth, where moths and rust destroy, and robbers break in and steal. Instead, store up riches for yourselves in heaven, where moths and rust cannot destroy, and robbers cannot break in and steal. For your heart will always be where your riches are."

Matthew 6:19–21 (TEV)

Evelyn sat down and looked at the broken glass on the floor. She wondered why she wasn't more upset. To her surprise, she didn't feel like crying. In fact, she felt relieved.

That stemmed bowl had posed on the dining room buffet since her mother had died almost 35 years ago. She had used it 35 times in her own home and many times as a child. The dish was a traditional part of Thanksgiving dinner. Her mother always used it to serve cranberries, so she had done the same. The dish had belonged to her mother's grandmother, and her mother would relate the origin of the dish each Thanksgiving. Then she would instruct the children to pass it carefully. Evelyn had done the same with her children.

Today she had bumped the dish with the handle of her dust mop. It lay in pieces on the floor. Evelyn thought she should be angry with herself. She thought she should blame herself for getting old and careless. She didn't feel that way. She just sat down and looked at the shattered glass on the floor.

Evelyn wanted to pass the dish to her grand-daughter, Jamie. She had planned to give it to Jamie when she came home from college for Thanksgiving. It would give her a chance to talk about another subject with Jamie.

Jamie didn't go to church anymore—not that Jamie's father (Evelyn's son) went as much as he should either. Evelyn had learned long ago not to interfere in the lives of her family. But she could tell Jamie what it meant to have a family heirloom. The dish was not just a pretty piece of glassware for serving cranberries. It reminded her of how her parents and grandparents had nurtured her faith. She had planned to say, "I'm giving you this dish, Jamie, but you don't have to serve cranberries in it. That's all in the past. I hope you can use it like I did. I hope it will remind you of the faith in Jesus that has been part of our family for many generations." Evelyn had wondered if that was too pushy. But it made no difference. It was the truth, and it would be spoken in love.

Now the dish was broken. Was she relieved because now she wouldn't have to give that little speech to Jamie? No, that wasn't it. She'd have to change what she had planned to say. She had a couple of weeks to work on it. She thought the conversation might start something like this: "Jamie, I had planned to give you that stemmed serving dish from my great-grandmother— you know, the one we always used for cranberries at Thanksgiving. But I broke it a couple of weeks ago. I'm sorry. But then I began thinking. You're going to move around a lot in your life, and the last thing you need is an old dish that would make you feel guilty if you broke it or lost it. I broke it, but I don't feel guilty at all. You see, it was only a serving dish, though it reminded me of how my mother and grandmother told me stories about Jesus. They helped me know how much He loved me.

"Jamie, I want to give you something more than a dish. Things we collect on earth don't mean much. I threw away the pieces of the dish. In a sense, that was like having a funeral for my mother and grandmother. But it was different because the glass dish is gone while my mother and grandmother are living in heaven. That's what Jesus promised. You can carry His grace a lot easier than you could carry that cranberry dish. And it will last a lot longer."

Evelyn reached for the dustpan. She'd have to work on her speech a little more. But she knew she had a good start.

Prayer: Holy Spirit, thank You for my faith in Jesus Christ. Help me to pass this gift to others. Amen.

For Reflection

- Look around your room. What memories do you attach to favorite objects? How might these memories also help you remember God's love?

- Does anyone in your family need to be reminded of God's love through Jesus? What can you do to remind them?

Eldon Weisheit

"If It Weren't for the Nights"

Sleep clinics do a thriving business. Many Americans don't get enough rest. "Tell me about it!" you say.

A night of tossing and turning leaves us groggy and listless the next morning. Several factors contribute to this affliction: inappropriate or too much medication, too many naps during the day, and too many things on our minds.

An ancient prayer of the church went like this: "From ghoulies and ghosties and long-legged beasties and things that go *thump* in the night, good Lord, deliver us." It was the prayer for All Hallows' Eve—Halloween to us. It arose at a time of rampant belief in ghosts and evil spirits.

Having brightened our dark nights with megawatts of light, we insist that no such evil spirits lurk in the darkness. We're much too sophisticated for that. But that doesn't make us sleep any better.

Most distressing are those thoughts that awaken

pangs of guilt and shame. We remember a thoughtless word, a careless comment, an act of unkindness that hurt the feelings of a friend or neighbor. Perhaps it was something that happened long ago when someone didn't get invited to a family wedding. Whatever it was, we're unable to shake the thoughts from our minds. The night gets longer and darker and deeper.

A patient at Lutheran Hospital in St. Louis, Mo., was scheduled for relatively simple surgery—gallbladder removal. He was terribly restless, thrashing about his bed and roaming the hospital corridors. Still, no sleep came.

Finally, a nurse called me. As the chaplain, I came into the semidarkened room and said, "I hear you're having trouble getting to sleep."

"I sure am," the man said. Then he poured out a story that had been part of his life for more than 50 years. "Chaplain, my wife and I have a beautiful marriage. It's the most precious thing we share with one another. But something keeps bugging me, especially tonight as I think about the operation tomorrow. Long ago, before I met my wife, I dated a young lady. We became too deeply involved in our relationship ... if you know what I mean. The trouble is that I've never told my wife about it, and it makes me feel so dirty that I just can't get it out of my head."

"Sounds like this was on your mind for a long time," I said.

"It sure was, and it keeps coming up at night. I just can't shake it." After talking about the incident of more than 50 years ago, we got to talking about his spiritual life—Baptism, confirmation, first communion. We talked about Jesus—who He is and what He meant to this man. We talked about grace, forgiveness, mercy, and the love of God. Then we celebrated Holy Communion. The man relaxed. "Well, I guess I'm ready for sleep. Good night. Thanks for coming."

He went to sleep and awoke a "new person," the nurse said. "What did you do to him?" she asked me the next day.

"We talked about Jesus, about his Baptism and confirmation. Then we celebrated Holy Communion," I replied.

"That was all?" the nurse said. "I should have thought of that myself!"

Psalm 130 has good words for restless nights plagued with guilt. "Out of the depths I cry to You, O LORD; O Lord, hear my voice. Let Your ears be attentive to my cry for mercy. If You, O LORD, kept a record of sins, O Lord, who could stand? But with You there is forgiveness; therefore You are feared. I wait for the LORD, my soul waits, and in His word I put my hope" (Psalm 130:1–5).

Martin Luther suffered from a guilt-driven conscience. He wrote, "I know what happens to me when I call to mind the previous actions of my whole life. For even though I know that my sins are forgiven ... I cannot be without sobs ... I am certainly not conscious of defiling another man's wife, of murder, or similar enormous crimes. In this respect the little dog cannot bite me, but he bites me again in respect to other sins, even though conscience has been healed and the scar closed up" (*Luther's Works,* Vol. 6, p. 371).

So what shall we do when we can't sleep because of a troubled conscience? Hymns such as "What a Friend We Have in Jesus" or "Amazing Grace" will help. Maybe it's also time to seek out a trusted friend, a pastor or elder, someone who will listen without scolding you or saying, "Oh, lots of people have done worse!" Another person's sins will not quiet your conscience.

Above all be assured that "Where sin increased, grace increased all the more, so that, just as sin reigned in death, so also grace might reign through righteousness to bring eternal life through Jesus Christ our Lord" (Romans 5:20–21).

Prayer: Lord Jesus, thank You for taking away my sins. I often don't forgive myself as completely as You forgive me. Give me strength and freedom to enjoy Your forgiveness. Amen.

For Reflection

- Plan ahead. Memorize Psalm 130:3–4. When do you think you might use these verses?
- Suppose you were advising someone who couldn't accept God's forgiveness. What would you say?

Martin Brauer

Angels of Welding

But the angel said to them, "… I bring you good news of great joy."

Luke 2:10

Angels were all around when I was little. They didn't come inside me, as did God. Angels were around people. They rode fenders on my father's car. They sat still beside my mother. They leaned over us when we were ill. Angels helped us sing louder and made it possible to remember something we didn't want to forget. Angels knew where we were at all times. They didn't talk like God and didn't know as much as Jesus, but angels knew more than any human, and there was a good reason to trust them—their boss was God.

Recently I agreed to write with children a family book on angels. First, I read about attributes of angels. These are phrases I found: Angels highlight what God does. They praise, vibrate, sing, light, glorify, serve, fly, carry news, bring messages, come and go, disappear,

appear in outer realms, come in dreams, startle, amaze, give awe.

Then I did what my children and I had done years ago. I said to the children who were helping me, "Close your eyes and I will tell you a story, read you a poem, tell you a picture. Look with both eyes closed, then draw what you see." (How often my children and I had played this game. I still do.) The children drew more than I told or saw.

I walked between their drawings. I saw yellow, green, and golden halos. I saw angels playing drums and violins. The space for angels was the open space of nature. The children found room for angels in any distance, near or far. I asked what they saw as the ministry of angels. Most of all, children saw angels stopping bullets, turning fighter planes around in midair. Angels held bullet-proof wings against armies and told submarines, "Stop!"

Now I could write. One of my many new poems is about Welding Angels. I think of mountains of metal poured into weapons. I know the fun of welding, making scrap metal beautiful, shaping flowers from broken fenders. Read my poem. What do you see?

If Angels of Welding would clean up a war,
they'd melt down the guns and set up a store
with roses of iron and tulips of steel,
while barrels of guns would be rod and a reel.

The bombers and fighters and engines that roar
would melt into puddles and be iron ore.

If Angels of Welding would finish a war,
they'd melt down the cruisers and set up a store
with lilies of metal and violets of brass
and grind down the bulkheads and bury the glass.

They'd take hand grenades and cut them in half
and turn them to bracelets to make children laugh.
Submarines, buried in oceans so deep,
would jump high with dolphins and leap when
  they leap.

If Angels of Welding would visit a war,
they'd soon stop the fighting and set up a store
with ice cream and chocolate to patch up each space
where war and bombardments did open some place.

The angels would take broken pieces apart,
weld war into roses or into a heart.

Imagine peace. Picture peace as you pray. Picture peace so you feel God's power.

Prayer: O God, give us images of angels making peace. Help us look at peaceful times in life more than we look at the times of hurt and war and pain. Show us the power and joy of Your peace. In Jesus' name we pray. Amen.

For Reflection

- Close your eyes and think the word *peace.* What pictures do you see? Ask a child to do the same.

- Have you ever thought of angels welding? What other unusual things might you imagine angels doing?

Herbert Brokering

Wherever

Read Matthew 16:24–28; Psalm 82; and focus on the following: "I will follow You wherever You go."

Luke 9:57

Once you hear Jesus reveal the Good News of salvation, once your God-given faith latches on to what He has done, once you yearn to obey His law of love, then it's going to happen: You want to follow. You want to follow Him wherever He goes.

Jesus is surrounded by companions. You and I are among them. You couldn't count how many have walked with Jesus through the centuries. Just to be with Him, to hear Him speak, is to be reckoned among the great privileges of life. Christian discipleship, however, is not just being *with* Jesus for a while and hearing Him.

You take something of a risk when you join the company of Christ. You risk ending up in the "followship" of Christ. This risk became an issue for three casual pedestrians in Jesus' entourage (Luke 9:57–62). One of them confidently declared, "I will follow You wherever You go." Jesus responded by pointing out what following him would entail.

Occasional membership has no place in Jesus' company. To follow Jesus means to turn away from and let loose of your former life. It means being tied to Jesus. It means accepting all Christ has done for you and responding to His love in all that you do. It's the risk you take when you "walk along the road" with Jesus.

The Christian church, in whose fellowship we walk, does not exist simply to render a heavenly glow over our earthly existence. The church has a publicly declared aim to awaken in people an irresistible desire to become Jesus' disciples, accepting whatever the consequences might be to follow Jesus wherever He leads.

Maybe you have escaped any such desire, though you have been sitting in the "congregation of the righteous" for years. Are you ready to respond to the risk? Don't say you haven't been warned. Every time you step into church, every time you seat yourself at Jesus' feet to hear His Word, every time you read Scripture, you run the risk that Jesus may spark in you an irresistible urge to follow Him.

If you think you can be an active disciple and still manage to keep day-to-day life as it is, forget that. To follow Christ does not plant your feet on a broad and comfortable way. The way is hard and long and narrow. It's full of demands and privations. Discipleship doesn't make life easier. If you're excessively concerned with a manicured lawn, an arbored patio, or even a roof over your head, following Christ may not be acceptable to you. I'm not just making this up. Jesus said it. "Foxes have holes and birds of the air have nests, but the Son of Man has no place to lay His head" (Luke 9:58). Those who follow Him are likely to experience some cold and sleepless nights. I don't want to scare you off. It's simply the way things are. But far from being impossibly demanding, when you remember with whom you walk, I'd say the experience is glorious.

Prayer Suggestion: Renew your confirmation pledge and ask the Holy Spirit to help you remain faithful to Jesus, even to the point of death (Revelation 2:10).

For Reflection

- List three personal experiences where following Jesus was easy and rewarding.
- List three personal experiences where following Jesus was difficult and awkward.

Arnold Kuntz

"Still Full of Sap and Green!"

Remember the last months, even the last couple of years, before retirement? We looked forward to that day—no more schedules, alarm clocks, or cantankerous bosses to keep happy. What a life! Retirement, we're ready for it! The sooner, the better. Early retirement, that would be the best of all worlds— a couple of years with nothing but fishing and golf and maybe a part-time job at the hardware store or bakery.

For some people, retirement comes too soon. The company downsizes—that's a new word to old-timers— and the management says they've got to cut the budget. Maybe they offer a generous bonus. Maybe they'll use you as a consultant when there's a special project. (You knew all along they couldn't get along without you!) You accept with thanks the gold watch, the fishing gear, and the other trinkets.

What's going on? It doesn't make sense to eliminate workers with wisdom and a lifetime of know-how. People of faith sense that something's not right. But who are we to complain?

Society has accepted the notion that 65, or sometimes 71, is the magic age for people to drop out of productive life. The result is that we really don't expect anything from the "elderly," no matter how "elderly" they are. We who are the elderly have sometimes taken the bait also.

An African proverb says, "When an old person dies, a valuable library burns to the ground." Our challenge is to hang on to these human tomes, these "books" of wisdom and stories of past generations. They are too precious to lose. We can apply a biblical statement to the plight of those who remain productive past retirement age. They represent the words of Psalm 92:12–15: "The righteous will flourish like a palm tree, they will grow like a cedar of Lebanon; planted in the house of the LORD, they will flourish in the courts of our God. They will still bear fruit in old age, they will stay fresh and green, proclaiming, 'The LORD is upright; He is my Rock.'" The Revised Standard Version has a livelier translation of verse 14: "They still bring forth fruit in old age, they are green and full of sap."

"Green and full of sap"! That doesn't describe couch potatoes. The Creator knows nothing of retirement, of downsizing His kingdom's action. Of course, we aren't as energetic as we once were. Age and illness take a lot from the best of us. But as long as life remains in our bodies, we are on the Lord's payroll. Payroll not in the sense that He rewards us according to our productivity; rather, His blessings last day and night, forever.

Eventually, years take their toll. Ecclesiastes 12:1 offers this cautionary note: "Remember your Creator in the days of your youth, before the days of trouble come and the years approach when you will say, 'I have no pleasure in them.'" Even through many losses, the energy we need to serve God does not drain away.

Ada was 98 years old. Her 35-year-old grandson was killed in an air disaster. At first her tears were bitter, almost resentful that she was still living when this precious young grandson was dead. She talked about what was going on around her, specifically in the four-bed room in which she now lived. She said at least six roommates had died in the past year. She remembered each of them. She talked about pulling the call light when one of her friends needed help. Every night she prayed the Lord's Prayer aloud with them. As she talked, she looked the chaplain straight in the eye. She knew just why she was still alive. She was truly full of sap and green. In her 98th year, she was bearing the fruit of the Spirit.

Sometimes it takes a little imagination to find what the Lord enables you to do. One thing remains certain: You are full of the Holy Spirit, full of the joy of living in Jesus' name.

Prayer: Dear Holy Spirit, I'm still green and full of sap. Use me to serve the Father through service to those in need. Amen.

For Reflection

- What can't you do now for the Lord that you could do before?

- What can you do now for the Lord that you couldn't do before?

Martin Brauer

Subtracting by Adding

Read Genesis 2:15–16; 3:1–3

Children are known to embellish their mother's words with fanciful, grim additions. Mom's request that big sister check on what her little brother is doing comes out, "Mom said you better stay in our yard—and get your tricycle off the driveway—or you'll be sent to your room with no dessert tonight!"

When challenged about the way she "improved" on mother's concern, big sister innocently explains that she did it for her brother's good: Dad might run over the tricycle left in the driveway and leaving the yard is dangerous for a 3-year-old. Big sister's excusing commentary is law-oriented puffery. In truth, it's what she thought Mom should have said.

Eve would have made a wonderful "big sister." Did you pick up on that from the readings? If you didn't, read them again. Slowly. Note what Eve added. Eve's addition is a truth of a sorts. In her logical mind, nothing bad would have happened if no one had touched the forbidden fruit. But God didn't say, "Don't touch." Eve did. The advice went beyond God's command.

Big deal? I think so. Let your mind work back across the years. Think of all the "rules" that families and churches have evolved in the name of God that reflect opinion more than His revealed will. I'll name a few: no movies on Sunday, no dancing, no card playing, wear hats in church, no lipstick on communion Sundays. Some of these may sound like God's Word, but they aren't. Is it wrong to embellish God's Word?

Wrong? Absolutely. It's idolatry that equates human words with the voice of God in matters where He is silent. It's the sinful opposite of spurning His Word and ridiculing what He says. A second problem in adding to God's Word is that we attack the freedom Christ gave us (Galatians 5:1). In wide areas of life, God gives Christians liberty to serve His purposes in ways of their individual choosing. He lets us work out how faith in Him best worships Him and serves human needs.

When there is a disruption of the social order, it seems people try to draw God into the middle of the debate—on their side. So what is God's position on women's rights? Social Security? NATO? Public education? The distribution of wealth? Working mothers? Registration of firearms? I've watched faces redden to a life-threatening hue as they debate the "proper" location of the pulpit, the use of the common cup for Holy Communion, and whether we should read from an RSV or an NIV Bible. They add what they think God would have said had He spoken on the subject.

Why not make a list to display on your refrigerator door—your own 95 Theses. Entitle the list: "Things God Has Clearly Said." Look for things God has actually said. Examples are John 3:16–17. Ephesians 2:8–10. At the top of my list is Romans 8:28. It doesn't say everything is good. It says God is at work in my life, and His purpose there is to make things _____.

Now there's a thought to keep an old man going all day long—and beyond! I'll bet older women like it too.

Prayer: Heavenly Father, keep me faithful to Your Word. Help me know the difference between what You have inspired and what people have created. Thank You for giving us Your clear Word. Amen.

For Reflection

- What "religious rules" can you cite? Which are God's Word, and which are human?
- How would you tactfully talk with someone who tried to convince you that God's Word includes something it doesn't include?

Charles S. Mueller Sr.

Celebrating Life by Celebrating Faith

I sn't it great to be alive? Even with pains, aches, worries, and empty days, we can and we do rejoice that the Lord is still the Lord of hope, joy, and peace.

Remember the line, "At my age, I've seen it all, I've heard it all, I've done it all—I just can't remember it all"? This may be true for many of us, but one thing we can remember and rejoice about is that the Lord remains the Lord of our life.

Another quote warns: "Be nice to your kids—they'll choose your nursing home for you." Another statement I heard from some parents of teenagers: "Was St. Paul kidding when he said, 'All things work together for good'? He must not have had any kids!"

Life is to be celebrated—even in the dark days. What comfort to know that after every bad day, there's always an Easter! God promises this! On days when you and I struggle to celebrate life, on days when things aren't going well, on days when we remember the sign "In case of an accident—I'm not surprised," we are comforted by the presence of the Spirit who points us to the cross and the empty tomb.

We celebrate life by celebrating our faith! I need Easter people around me on dark days. When I am flying as high as an Easter person, I share my joy in the Lord with those who are having sin-stained Good Friday days.

Look around you. Who is unhappy and suffering? How can you share the joy of Easter with them? Keep looking. Who are the Easter people in your life? How can you connect with them so their Easter joy rubs off on you?

People of God know that our Lord continues to send His Spirit to us to give us hope and joy. God loves us unconditionally, just as we are and not as we should be. That's the hope we have in the Lord!

Celebrate today as a gift from the Lord. Remember the comforting words of Jeremiah 29:11: " 'For I know the plans I have for you,' declares the LORD, 'Plans to prosper you and not to harm you, plans to give you hope and a future.' "

Our future is filled with hope and joy. The future that looked so fatal on Good Friday has dissolved into the Easter Sonrise. Our future is now. Have a great day of celebrating your faith with those around you!

Prayer Suggestion: Thank the Lord for the gift of today. Ask Him to send Easter people into your life.

For Reflection

- How can you share your life with two special people this week?
- Ask two other people to help you celebrate their life in a special way this week.

Rich Bimler

The Young for the Old
and
the Old for the Young

Nuclear families have replaced extended families. More often than not, families live many miles from each other. We who remember Christmas, Thanksgiving, birthdays, and anniversaries as times for family gatherings feel deeply the loss of celebrations canceled by distance.

Jesus lived with an extended family. There were cousins, sisters, brothers, aunts, uncles, and grandparents. With Jesus and His earthly family, it was truly "the young for the old and the old for the young."

Jesus took seriously the care of Mary, His mother. Scholars conjecture that Jesus' earthly father, Joseph, might have died while He was young, assuming that Joseph was older than Mary. St. John tells the tender story of Jesus caring for His mother even as He languished on the cross.

Near the cross of Jesus stood His mother,
His mother's sister, Mary the wife of Clopas,
and Mary Magdalene. When Jesus saw
His mother there, and the disciple whom
He loved standing nearby, He said to His
mother, "Dear woman, here is your son,"
and to the disciple, "Here is your mother."
From that time on, this disciple took her
into his own home. John 19:25–27

Today, intergenerational life is difficult to foster. The traditional shape of family life has disappeared. We hear that people today don't care for one another as they once did. But recent studies show that huge numbers of Americans are now involved in caregiving—far more than in the past. At any one time, 20 percent of American households have at least one individual providing full-time care. One adult in nearly a quarter of the country's households has been involved in unpaid caregiving for someone age 50 or over. (These figures are from a survey conducted jointly by National Alliance for Caregiving and AARP.) So the challenge is "How do we help one another?"

Just as we learned to live with and help our children grow, so now we learn to live with ourselves and older family members as we move relentlessly from one age to the next. We learn from Jesus, our teacher. He cared for His mother, and when He could no longer be present, He provided for her care through John. It was a terrible moment for Jesus. Not only was He suffering the pain of crucifixion, but He also felt rejected by the people He loved. At one point, His heavenly Father turned His face away from Him. Still Jesus provided help for His mother.

Jesus helps us to care and shows us how. He was a faithful son to His mother. "Here is your mother," He says to friend John. That was all John needed. He immediately accepted responsibility for protecting Mary.

God has blessed us with more resources than people in our situation had 50 or 60 years ago. Jesus still cares for our elders through us, and He graciously equips us for the task. Jesus' death on the cross and His resurrection enable to do what He asks—to be kind and loving caregivers. Jesus' death on the cross and His resurrection give us the energy and will to care. He also forgives our moments of thoughtlessness.

What does the Christian faith say about the care of self, parents, and spouse? It says what it always has said. Your times are in God's hands. Trust and be not afraid. Let hope keep you joyful. In trouble be patient. When you pass through the deep waters, God will be with you. Rest in the Lord, wait patiently for Him, and you will yourself be joy and refreshment to those for whom you care.

Prayer Suggestion: Speak clearly and openly to the Lord. Talk about the really human needs with which you are dealing. He will not let you down.

For Reflection

- What specific care can you realistically provide for those older than you?
- What care can you accept from elderly people who are younger than you?

Martin Brauer

Celebrating
the Majors

B ack in the 1960s, I was on a public university campus. A friend had asked me to locate his son, who had expressed interest in attending the seminary. I met the young man, and I asked, "What's your major?" He hesitated a moment, smiled, then said, "I guess I've actually majored in minors—mostly sleeping, arguing with the administration, and playing golf." (I resisted the temptation to suggest that at least two of the three minors had potential value in preparation for being a preacher!)

"Majoring in minors" fascinated me. I know it isn't only during the college years that we major in minors. As I look back over my life, I feel that I have at many times majored in minors.

When I visited with a friend for the first time after he was diagnosed with terminal cancer, I initiated talk about what the doctors had said, how he felt, and how he slept and ate. When I asked him if he'd like to pray, he immediately answered yes. I asked what he'd like to pray about, and I was surprised when he said, "That I never spent as much time and effort with my family as I should have." As we met at other times, I saw how God healed my friend of his guilt. God also forgave him for majoring in the minors. I also saw how the Lord brought the family closer together.

As we grow older, we are still tempted to major in minors—to spend a lot of time and energy on unimportant things. We give disproportionate time to minors. It might be concern about our status, destructive gossip or criticism, or watching television. We easily fail to respond to major opportunities for serving our Lord. Also, we can easily make majors out of little things that annoy or worry us—the habits of young people, what we feel as a loss of power, and little things about our family or our church.

What is the positive side? In what should we major? Jesus says in Matthew 6:33: "Seek first His kingdom and His righteousness, and all these things will be given to you as well." Paul writes in Philippians 3:13: "One thing I do: Forgetting what is behind and straining toward what is ahead, I press on toward the goal to win the prize for which God has called me heavenward in Christ Jesus."

When we examine our majors, we ask ourselves, "Is this glorifying God in His kingdom? Is this moving toward the goal—the prize—as a child of God?"

Some of you may say, "These are good, pious statements, but isn't it true that different people have different majors at different times? Isn't it true that two Christians can approach the question of what is a major for God's kingdom in a given situation and come up with two different answers?" The answer to both questions, of course, is yes. However, these complications also support the basic messages of God's kingdom: God loves us. He redeemed us. However, we still possess human limitations. We're still sinful. We're still tempted to major in minors, and we often succumb. But God actively participates in our lives. He's here to bless us, show us His will, reveal both the majors and the minors, and show us the perfect way.

We have many advantages in knowing what constitutes the majors. As we review our lives, we see again what is important. We're likely to remember an enjoyable day with our children, but we have trouble recalling any details from frustrations we had at work. We can share this hindsight with young people.

What is our role now? It's to celebrate and enjoy God's love. We enjoy God's love when we rest in His hands, relax in His care, quit trying to make minors into majors, and accept His will and guidance. How? Through His grace. God forgave our sins of making minors into majors. He guides us to identify majors and helps us overcome the temptation to major in minors. God leads us to seek first His kingdom and His righteousness. He's there to bless us. With His guidance we can see, seek, and rejoice in the majors.

Prayer Suggestion: Ask the Lord to help you concentrate on the majors. Thank Him for putting these blessings and opportunities into your life.

For Reflection

- List the most important (major) things in your life. Check your list regularly. Do you have a proper focus? What struggles do you anticipate?

- Where do you see others majoring in the minors? What can you do about it?

Les Bayer

Check Your ID

[God said,] "Fear not, for I have redeemed you; I have called you by your name; You are Mine."

Isaiah 43:1b (NKJV)

Get out your driver's license or some other identification card. Don't worry if you no longer have an ID card—that may help prove my point. For now, join me in thinking about things that help identify you.

Your name is the first item needed for identification. Is the name on your ID card the same name you use with family and friends? Do you have a middle name or initial that you only use on demand for some official document? Do you have a nickname that is not on your card? Your parents, brothers, and sisters may have had a special name for you. My wife calls me *honey* much more often than she calls me *Eldon*. I suppose that's true for many married couples. As grandparents we like the names our children's children call us, even if it is some corny title like *Boompa*.

God is big on names. Soon after creating Adam, He gave the first human the job of name-giver. God Himself named many people, and He often changed people's names to show them and others that their status had changed. What do you think God calls you? Does He use the name your parents gave? Has He kept up with your name changes? Or does He have a special name for you? Whatever the case, God knows you by name. He does not now, nor will He in the future, need an introduction.

Just as the name others call you indicates their relationship to you, God reveals His relationship to you by what He calls you. When you were baptized, God identified Himself as the one who created you, the one who became your brother to save you, and the one who gave you new life. Because we call God names such as Father, Son, and Holy Spirit, we can understand something about what He calls us. We are His children because He created us. We are His saints because Christ has forgiven us. We are united with one another because the Holy Spirit calls us together.

Now think about another item on your ID card—your address. You may have had many addresses. Many older people like to recall events from their past by remembering where they lived at the time. The places they lived became part of their identity. Where you have lived helps explain who you are.

Now do a fast forward. When Jesus explained why He was leaving His disciples, He said He was going to prepare a place for them and He promised to return for them. That promise is also for us. Just as we identify our past by the places we have lived, we also know our future address because Jesus revealed it.

Look at the other things on your ID that have changed through the years. Color of hair? Height and weight, which have undoubtedly gone up—and sometimes started to go down again. The age has changed year by year. Even though such items are used to identify us, we recognize that we are who we are despite statistics that change regularly. If your ID includes your picture, take a closer look at it. Remember your pictures from confirmation, school yearbooks, your wedding, and other record-setting events. Those pictures chronicle phases of your history.

The changes on your identification card provide a good record of your life. Life naturally includes change. Only those who died young will not experience gray or disappearing hair. Only those who no longer have an address on earth are immune from the changes we experience.

You need not fear those changes. Look back to see how much your life has changed in the past 20, 40, or 60 years. Those changes helped you as you faced other changes. They will help you in the future too. They can serve as a reminder not only of who you are and where you live, but also whose you are and where you are going. You need not fear. God promised to care for you. And He never changes.

Swift to its close ebbs out life's little day;
Earth's joys grow dim, its glories pass away;
Change and decay in all around I see;
O thou who changest not, abide with me.

Prayer: Lord God, thank You for claiming me through the grace and love of Jesus Christ. Help me to live now with confidence that I will live with You forever. Amen.

For Reflection

- Can you remember or locate the oldest picture of yourself? The most recent? Compare them. Think of how God has cared for you in all the time between those pictures.

- If you made a time line of your life, what would you include as major milestones? Where does God's love and care fit in with each of those events?

Eldon Weisheit

The Authors

Les Bayer retired in Austin, Texas, after serving for 36 years as a college administrator and 10 years as an elementary school principal and teacher in the Lutheran education system. He founded and served as director of the Center for Urban Education Ministry. Les presently is an area representative for Wheat Ridge Ministries; tries to help his wife, Lois, with her social ministry volunteer activities; attempts to keep up with his eight grandchildren; and teaches elderhostels.

Shirley Bergman is the founder and director of the Lutheran Institute on Aging and the Family at Concordia University, Seward, Neb., which offers a nontraditional master's degree and continuing education programs in areas of family and aging. She serves as a speaker and leader at a variety of aging and family conferences and workshops. Her husband, Marvin, is a professor of Christian education at Concordia, Seward. They have two children and one grandson.

Rich Bimler serves as president of Wheat Ridge Ministries. He has also served as executive director of Youth Ministry for The Lutheran Church—

Missouri Synod, a district executive in Minnesota, and a director of Christian education in Kansas and Texas. He continues to enjoy life by playing with his five grandkids, keeping in close touch with his three kids, and gardening with his wife, Hazel. Some of his current books include: *Let There Be Laughter, Miracles in the Middle,* and *Angels Can Fly because They Take Themselves Lightly.*

Martin Brauer is a retired pastor who served parishes in Michigan, Missouri, and Tennessee. He is a certified chaplain and served at hospitals and nursing homes in Missouri. He has written worship materials published by Concordia Publishing House and Creative Communications for the Parish. He lives in St. Louis and has three children and eight grandchildren.

Roy Brockopp has been serving the church during his retirement as part-time manager of Older Adult Ministries for the Board of Human Care Ministries of The Lutheran Church—Missouri Synod. He has served as a parish pastor, administrator, lecturer, consultant, and trainer. He has hosted numerous radio programs. Roy and his wife, Ruth, continue to enjoy traveling to be with their four children and nine grandchildren.

Herbert Brokering serves as a staff associate for Wheat Ridge Ministries. He is a pastor, author, poet, international tour leader, as well as a popular speaker. He has written more than 30 books, plus lyrics for numerous anthems and songs. His newest books are: *I'm Thinking of You: Spiritual Letters of Hope and Healing* and *Angels Love Children: Stories, Poems, Prayers, and Other Family Fun.*

Ed Krueger attended Concordia (University) Teachers College, River Forest, Ill., and De Paul University. He served as teaching principal in Lutheran elementary schools in Indiana, Illinois, and Wisconsin, and as supervising teacher in Illinois. He served in the Northern Illinois District of The Lutheran Church—Missouri Synod as an executive in education, youth ministry, and evangelism. In retirement, he is involved in congregation, district, and community volunteer work. Ruth and Ed have three children and six grandchildren.

Arnold Kuntz has been active in The Lutheran Church—Missouri Synod, serving for 16 years as the president of the Pacific Southwest District and on the synodical Board of Directors. He also has served on the Board of Directors of Aid Association for Lutherans. He authored *Joy in the Journey,* a book of devotions for seniors, and *Keeping the Servant Spark,* encouragement for church workers.

Wayne Lucht was a Lutheran teacher for 43 years—15 years on the grade-school level and as principal and 28 years as a college professor at Concordia University, River Forest, Ill. During the last four years of college teaching and six more of semiretirement, Wayne served as editor of *Lutheran Education.*

August Mennicke served as pastor in parishes in Minnesota and Alabama, followed by several decades in the Minnesota North District office and The Lutheran Church—Missouri Synod headquarters in St. Louis. From 1995 until 1998, he was "repositioned" as senior pastor at St. Paul's, Des Peres, Mo. He has since retired from that position. He and his wife have five kids and 11 awesome grandkids. He has served as chairman of The Lutheran Church—Missouri Synod Council of Presidents and on the board of the American Bible Society.

Fred A. Meyer, a retired professor from Concordia College, Bronxville, N.Y., has served as teacher and principal in Lutheran schools, a writer and editor for the Board of Parish Services of The Lutheran Church—Missouri Synod, and a professor of education both at McKendree College and Concordia Bronxville. He is father to eight and grandfather to 14. He assists in the adult education program at Concordia, Kirkwood, Mo., and writes for *The Good Shepherd,* a magazine for the Christian home.

Charles S. Mueller Sr. has spent his life trying to become a caring husband, a responsible father, an effective pastor, and now, an interesting grandfather. All of this is still a work in progress energized by hope. Current free time is spent writing and helping congregations, families, and fellow seniors under the auspices of Wheat Ridge Ministries while filling in at Trinity, Roselle, Ill., as needed.

Dorothy Schultz, Slingerlands, N.Y., recently retired after 22 years teaching kindergarten in Bronxville, N.Y. During that time, she authored devotional materials for teachers, chapel services, and Christmas programs, as well as tunes and texts for her classroom and school. Her song texts have been published in musical compositions by her husband, Dr. Ralph C. Schultz, in *Little Ones Sing Praise* (Concordia Publishing House) and in *Lutheran Education.* She and Ralph joyfully share five children and ten grandchildren.

Frank Starr (associate editor) is pastor of First Lutheran Church, Lufkin, Texas. He previously served on the staff of *The Lutheran Witness* and has written or edited several books and Bible studies for Concordia Publishing House. He and his wife, Ann, have two children.

Eldon Weisheit was taken to heaven very suddenly by our Lord on Jan. 20, 1998, just a few months after he had retired and had written the devotions for this book. Eldon spent 35 years in the professional ministry—the last 20 at Fountain of Life, Tucson, Ariz. A prolific writer, Eldon's most recent books are *Aging Parents, Sharing Life's Defining Moments,* and *I Take out the Garbage because I Love You* (written with his wife, Carolyn).